SERPENT AND SIVA WORSHIP

AND MYTHOLOGY IN CENTRAL AMERICA, AFRICA, AND ASIA AND THE ORIGIN OF SERPENT WORSHIP

(1877)

Hyde Clake

and

C. Staniland Wake

ISBN 0-7661-0472-9

SERPENT AND SIVA WORSHIP

AND

MYTHOLOGY,

IN

CENTRAL AMERICA, AFRICA, AND ASIA.

AND

THE ORIGIN OF SERPENT WORSHIP.

Two Treatises.

BY

HYDE CLARKE, M.A.I.,

AND

C. STANILAND WAKE, M.A.I.

EDITED
BY
ALEXANDER WILDER, M. D.

NEW YORK:
J. W. BOUTON, 706 BROADWAY.
1877.

PREFACE.

THE researches and explorations of travelers, scientists and learned investigators, are every day adding to our knowledge of the Serpent-Cultus. It is rising above the old conception of an obscure and ill-defined superstition, to the dimensions of a religion, distinctly outlined in its characteristic features, and by no means without a recondite metaphysical basis. Not only did the children of Israel burn incense to the symbolical animal from Moses till Hezekiah, but the Hamitic races "from Memphis to Babylon," and all indeed at the far East and remote West, who accepted as sacred, what Mr. Brown denominates, "The Great Dionysiak Myth."

> "From India's coral strand,
> Where Afric's sunny fountains
> Roll down their golden sand ;
> From many an ancient river,
> From many a palmy plain,"

to the beech and birch forests of Scandinavia and the Frozen Ocean, and the remotest nooks of Polynesia and the American Continent, THE SERPENT, in all his forms, with hood, horns, or rattles, has been venerated by the various tribes of men as a god! If he conducted to the tree of prohibited knowledge in the garden of Eden, he was also an Æsculapius, the healer of men in the wilderness of Sinai, the good spirit of many a world-religion, the source of diviner inspiration, and the imparter of the highest, holiest, most essential life. Indeed, Serpent-lore is the literature of the earlier periods of ancient history.

The two papers of Messrs. Hyde Clarke and Staniland Wake, which are now reprinted from *The Journal of the Anthropological Institute of Great Britain and Ireland*, give a somewhat new direction to our studies of the subject. The latter gentleman, already well-known for his acuteness of perception and extraordinary synthetic powers, carries our attention to the prehistorical period, and seeks to portray the source and prevalence of serpent-worship among Medes, Akkadians and Scyths, in the very cradle of our race. Mr. Clarke, for many years an explorer of human origins, conducts us to the field of philology, and shows us *Siva*, who had been often imagined to be a subordinate divinity, and who was not known in the Vedic pantheon of the more ancient times, to be indeed a *maha deva*—not only the greatest god of ante-Brahman India, but also the First God of Africa, Western Asia, and Central America; the god who has, *par excellence*, the serpent for his symbol. He is Sibu, Shivatt, Kebê, Sabazios; and his seat is in the sky, at the very zenith, at the omphalos of the day. He is one and *The One;* the spirit which animates all nature, and of which every man is a manifestation. Before the *Veda* he was Buddha, the source of wisdom rather than its revelator.

Both Messrs. Clarke and Wake have conducted us into the arena of ethnical science, and open a door for inquiry, which will not be shut till the forgotten past is made to divulge its secrets.

The importance of such studies is becoming more generally acknowledged; and the scholar who adds to our information is regarded as a benefactor. The breadth of view which is afforded by the increase of knowledge is attended by enlargement of the scope of faculty, and so eventually there ensues a completer culture, greater intellectual vigor, and a more perfect ideal humanity.

New York, May 14, 1877.

INTRODUCTION.

"*Chil.* . . The Prince of Elder Time, be he God
Or Dæmon, Savior or Destroyer,
Is capable for all : speak more plainly.
B. M. Hear, then. I am *Maha Deva*,
God in the remotest East ; my throne
Is on the sacred Kailas, mount of the assembly;
My votaries, the black men of the Indian groves,
My worship, the oldest cult of men.
All peoples and all faiths are mine;
The hopes, passions, lusts and purposes of men
Are inspired by me and led on to success.
Ere the white Aryan invaded my forests,
And Brahman fanatics o'erturned my altars,
My children had crossed the Erythrean sea—
And I was the tutelar god of Babel,
The Dionysos of fertile Arabia,
Moloch in Syria, Baal in Tyre,
Hercules, who guided the Phœnician ships
To distant seas, and to the gardens
Of the Hesperides—or wheresoe'er
The mariners cared to go;
And everywhere I was revered and worshipped,
At the Baal-fires, Druid-groves, in caves
And remote places. . . Here I am called
The Black Man of the Forest,
And denounced as Satan, Prince of Evil."

"The serpent is not only monstrous and maleficent in Hindu tradition, but also at once the learned one, and he who imparts learning; it sacrifices itself to let the hero carry away the water of life, the water of strength, the health-giving herb or the treasure; it not only spares but it favors the predestined hero; it destroys individuals, but preserves the species; it devours nations, but preserves the regenerative kings; it poisons plants, and throws men into deep sleep, but it gives new strength in its occult domain to the sun, who gives new life to the world every morning and every spring. . . Hence the worship in India of the serpent, who is revered as a symbol of every species of learning."*

THE remains of Serpent-worship are to be found in all quarters of the earth, among nations geographically remote from each other, and supposed to be distinct in characteristics of race,

* DE GUBERNATIS: *Zoological Mythology*, part III., v. 405.

habitude, intellectual constitution and religious belief. Some faiths, like that of the Buddhists—perhaps the oldest of all,—still maintain a qualified veneration for the sacred animal as a part of their worship; while others, even among the more modern, do not hesitate to display the serpent-symbol conspicuously among their ecclesiastical decorations. We see it in the architecture of churches, and even find its reliques in the garb of priests. Moses is recorded as having erected the symbol of the Phœnician Æsculapius, the sun-god of autumn, as "a sign of salvation." The like device was borne upon the respective standards of the Assyrians, the Persians, the Romans, and even the British. It was thus honored by Christians as well as "heathen." Whole sects, we are assured by the early fathers, used to partake of the Eucharistical Supper, after it had been consecrated by a living snake coming from a coffer and entwining its coils about the loaves of bread.

Not only did it enter into the symbolical and ritual service of every religion in which the worship of the sun constituted the prominent feature, but we find it in countries where that worship appears to have been comparatively or altogether unknown, as in ancient Sarmatia, Scandinavia, and upon the Gold Coast of Africa. In every known country of the ancient world the serpent formed a prominent object of veneration, and made no inconsiderable figure in legendary and astronomical mythology. Its consecration as a religious emblem preceded the later forms of polytheism; and we find it in sacred legends of every country, in almost every temple, symbolizing almost every deity, imaged in the heavens, stamped upon the earth, and finally made supreme in the realms of everlasting sorrow.* "No nations were so geographically remote, or so religiously discordant, but that one—and only ONE—superstitious characteristic was common to all; that the most civilized and the most barbarous bowed down with the same devotion to the same engrossing deity; and that this deity either *was*, or was *represented by* the same SACRED SERPENT." Its antiquity must be accredited to a period far antedating all history.†

A symbolism so uniform as well as peculiar must be regarded as affording plausible evidence that the people employing it were of kindred ethnical origin. "Of all researches that most effectually aid us to discover the origin of a nation or people

* REV. JOHN BATHURST DEANE, M. A.: *Worship of the Serpent*, chap. viii., p. 443.

† HENRY O'BRIEN: *The Round Towers of Ireland*, chap. xvi., p. 222. "The parent is always senior to the offspring, but it is not quite such a *truism* that 'the most ancient record of the history of the serpent-tempter is the book of *Genesis*.' Before a line of it was ever written, or its author ever conceived, the allegory of the serpent was propagated all over the world. *Temples constructed thousands of years prior to the birth of Moses bear the impress of its history.*"

whose history is involved in the obscurity of ancient times, none, perhaps, are attended with such important results as the analysis of their theological dogmas and their religious practices. To such matters mankind adhere with the greatest tenacity; which, though modified and corrupted in the revolution of ages, still retain features of their original construction, when language, arts, sciences and political establishments no longer preserve distinct lineaments of their ancient constitution."* This is astonishingly exemplified in the religion of India. Notwithstanding the revolutions of time and dominion, the distractions of foreign and civil wars, and, what is more usually fatal than these, the addition of allegorical fictions, its original features are still sufficiently recognisable to identify it with the worship which prevailed in ancient Egypt, on the plains of Assyria, in the valleys of Greece, among the nations around the Caspian and Euxine seas, and their kindred tribes in northwestern Europe.

But this rule, it is pleaded, can hardly be extended to the populations of the western hemisphere. Yet the Serpent was generally revered among them; it entered widely into their symbolical representations, and it had essentially the same signification as among the early nations of the Eastern Continent. But philology and physiology seem to prevent us from supposing that there existed any original identity of race. The ruins on the two continents have little in common. The teocallis of Mexico and the mounds of North America are different from the pyramids of Egypt, and the artificial hills and "high places" of the eastern world. The resemblance in the symbols of worship is only apparent, despite the plausible remark of Mr. Squier, that "it can hardly be supposed that a symbol strictly arbitrary could accidentally be chosen to express the same idea." Nevertheless, the dissimilarities which appear in emblems of the same character are strikingly conspicuous. The sacred serpents of the eastern continent were by preference the *cobra de capella* or hooded snake of India, and the uræus, or royal asp of Egypt. There were also "dragons" of other species, the prodigious size of which was often noted. The apocryphal chapters of the book of *Daniel* mention such an animal at Babylon, and Alexander visited one in his lair near Taxila. But the sacred serpent of America is generally, especially among the wandering tribes, the rattlesnake. Indeed, Mr. George R. Gliddon was so impressed with the diversities as to assert that they proved that there could have been no possible intercourse between the two continents three thousand years ago, as many had conjectured.

It has, however, been a favorite idea of anthropologists and other speculators on the subject of human origins, that the Old World had afforded a parentage for the population of the New. The ten lost tribes of Israel have been evoked from their hiding-

* McCulloh: *American Researches,* page 225.

places; and even a stray passage in the apocryphal book of *Esdras* has done great service to eke out authority.* The Druids of Britain are largely a creation of the fancy from the barest historical basis, yet they were not wrought into shape and dimensions with an equal endeavor. One imaginative writer, however, a clergyman of some repute, has dismissed the American savages, and through the magic of his fresh-nibbed pen, our so-called Anglo-Saxon race became lost Israelites unawares. The Abbe de Bourbourg went further still. He propounds the hypothesis of a submerged continent in the middle Atlantic, which connected or at least communicated with the Old World, and was populated by the Atlantians, in which race was included the Hispano-Iberians, Ligurians, Etruscans, Moors, North Africans and Egyptians. His views, however, do not meet a cheerful acceptance. Our modern savants, though tolerably willing to have "missing links" for ancestors, do not graciously accept in that relation either aboriginal Americans or African negroes.

But Mr. Hyde Clarke, an ethnologist of superior merit, seems to indicate the way open for the adoption of the Australian race and its fellows. In another treatise he propounds the opinion that "we have two streams, at least, of dark and white races departing from India, and affecting us [the English and Irish] in these islands, altogether apart from the influence of Celts and English." Prof. Huxley notes them more carefully; one of tall stature, with fair skin and blue eyes; the other of short stature, with dark hair and dark eyes. Sir Henry Rawlinson has indicated two such races in ancient Babylonia; the *Adamu*, Adamites or dark race; the other the *Sarku*, or light race. The Ceylonese have a tradition that Adima and Hiva, the parents of the dark race of India, once paradised on that island, but were persuaded by an evil spirit to leave it for the mainland, and were never permitted to return.

There is, however, a conflict of ethnologists about these dark races, the just determination of which would greatly facilitate a correct judgment of the origin and dissemination of the Serpent-Cultus. The school which is represented by Max Müller, the Rawlinsons and other scholars, hailing we believe from Oxford, would direct our attention to the *Turanians*. These, they say, occupied all Northern Asia and Europe, and were the aboriginal race in Hindustan, Asiatic Ethiopia, Chaldea and Babylonia. Mr. Ferguson accordingly suggests that serpent-worship "arose among a people of Turanian origin, the primæval inhabitants

* *II. Esdras*, xiii. 40–42. "These are the ten tribes which were carried away prisoners out of their own land in the time of Osea the king, whom Salmanasar, the king of Assyria, led away captive; and he carried them over the waters, and so came they into another land. But they took this counsel among themselves, that they would leave the multitude of the heathen and go forth into a farther country where never mankind dwelt; that they might there keep their statutes which they never kept in their own land."

who first settled on the banks of the Lower Euphrates, and that it spread thence as from a centre to every country or land of the Old World, in which a Turanian people settled."* If we are not mistaken in our geography, this would be in the region of Duni, at the confluence of the Tigris and Euphrates, called in the Assyrian tablets Kar-duniyas or Gan-duniyas. This latter name is the same as *GaN-EDeN*, the garden of God; and, indeed, Sir Henry Rawlinson has pointed out the agreement of the Babylonian region of Kar-duniyas with the Eden of the Bible.† This would make Mr. Fergusson's hypothesis square very well with the Biblical one, and perhaps sustain the theory of Mr. Robert Brown, Jr., in regard to the Great Dionysiak Myth, which seems to indicate the origin of Bacchus-worship and its inhering ophiolatry, in Sumir and Akkad in this same region. But the Adamites would thus be set down as a pretty inferior race of Mongol Tartars, hardly likely to develop a skilful and cultured stock like the family of Cain or the builders of the city and tower of Babel.

Mr. Wake's hypothesis is somewhat more explicit. He is of opinion that "Serpent-Worship, as a developed religious system, originated in Central Asia, the home of the great Scythic stock, from whom sprang all the civilized races of the historical period. These people are the *Adamites*, and their legendary ancestor was at one time regarded as the Great Serpent—his descendants being in a special sense serpent-worshippers."

But Adam, Mr. Wake suggests in another treatise, was not "the name given at first to this mythical father of the race." He suggests that the term was formed by the combination of the primitive Akkadian words AD, father, and DAM, mother. "It would thus," he remarks, "originally express a dual idea, agreeably to the statement in *Genesis* v. 2, that male and female were called 'Adam.' (This agrees perfectly with the Persian and other traditions which made the first human being androgynous or double-sexed.) When the dual idea expressed in the name was forgotten, Adam became the Great Father; the Great Mother receiving the name of Eve (Havvah), i. e., living or life" —(in Arabic, a serpent).

Mr. Wake accordingly, with much ingenuity, associates the Persians, Greeks and Romans, and probably the Hindus and Celtic people with the Medes of the earlier historical period, and through them with the Akkadians or Chaldeans of Babylonia. He gives the word *ak* the sense of "root or stem, lineage;" and so Ak-Ad would mean the sons of Ad or Adam. This would make the Chaldeans Adamites, and sustain the hypothesis of the original home in their country. The Mad [M-Ad] or Medians who established the first kingly government in the country, he

* FERGUSSON: *Tree and Serpent Worship*, Introductory Essay, part I. p. 3.

† *Forty-Sixth Report of the Royal Asiatic Society.*

suggests as the parent-stock from which the Akkadians were derived. Somewhat similar ideas exist in various regions. The Parsees of Hindustan have the legend of the great Ab-Ad, the first ancestor of mankind. The Hindu *purans* refer to the reign of King *It* or Ait, an avatar of Siva. Egypt was named Ait or Aëtos, from a king whom the Greek writers represent as a Hindu. The *purans* spoke of *Yadavas*, descendants of "Aëtus or Yatu," that emigrated to Abyssinia.* Yama, the Brahman god of the Underworld, associated or identified with Takshak, the king of the serpents, was regarded as the original progenitor of mankind. Hence it was his office to receive them after death, and to reward or punish them according to their merits.

The Arabs also had their ancestor Ad, and one of their tribes bore that designation. The Yezidis of Mesopotamia also venerrate Sheikh Adi, their Adam Kadmon or Ancient One, in whose honor they celebrate mysterious rites like those of the Korybantes of ancient Phrygia. Mr. Layard has preserved a hymn to this sacred personage which identifies him as divine, the architect of all things, preceding all that exists, self-originated, the One and Only One, the Ancient of days, receiving the highest wisdom from the Eternal Essence.† The Egyptians, likewise, venerated a similar divine being, denominated At-um or At-mu, the Father of mankind. He was the first-born or Only Son whom the Egyptians mourned in their orgies. He was identical with Adon or Tammuz of Syria, or Tamuzi of the Tablets, who was also annually mourned by the women of Western Asia at the sacred rites.

Mr. Wake now carries his genealogy from Hamites and Shemites to Aryans, and even to other people that we were beginning to consider as of different races. "It has now been shown that not only are the peoples mentioned in the *Toldoth Beni Noah* [genealogy of the sons of Noah] rightly classed his descendants of the mythical *Ad*, but that the Asiatic Aryans with the allied peoples of Europe to the farthest limits of the Celtic area, may also well be thus described. The ancient *Mad* [early Medians] belonged, however, to the great Scythic stock; and hence all the Turanian peoples, including the Chinese, may doubtless be classed among the Adamites." This would exclude perhaps the dark peoples of the tropics; but a way is made for

* "The name Ethiopia may be explained in like manner—*Ait* or *Aith*, the Indian *prince*, and *opia*, a common termination in the Mediterranean countries.

"In the *History of India* by Collonca-Batta, the following passage occurs: "Under the reign of Viswamitra, first king of the dynasty of *Soma Vansa* (the human race), in consequence of a battle which lasted five days, Manuvenna, heir of the ancient kings [of the Solar dynasty], abandoned by the Brahmans, emigrated with all his companions, passing through Arya [Iran] and the countries of Barria, till he came to the shores of Masra,"—Mitzra, or the Nile.

† LAYARD: *Nineveh and Babylon*, vol. I., iv.

the Mexican and kindred American peoples. The connecting link would seem to be our own Northern race. Says Mr. Wake: "One of the solar heroes of the *Volsung Tale* is ATLI, who becomes the second husband of Gudrun, the widow of Sigurd; Sigurd himself being the slayer of the dragon Fafnir, who symbolises the darkness or cold of a northern winter—the Vritra of Hindu mythology. This dragon-enemy of Indra was also called *Ahi*, the strangling snake, who appears again as *Atri;* and Mr. Cox supposes that the name *Atri* may be the same as *Atli* of the Volsung Tale. *Atli*, who in the *Nibelung Song* is called *Etzel*, overpowers the chiefs of Niflheim [the underworld], who refused to give up the golden treasures which Sigurd had won from the dragon, and he throws them into a pit full of snakes.

"The connection of the Teutonic hero with the serpent is remarkable, for in the Mexican mythology we meet with a divinity having almost the same name, and associated with the same animal. Humboldt tells us that the Great Spirit of the Toltecs was called *Teotl;* and Hardwicke says that *Teotl* was the Only-God of Central America. If so, however, he was a serpent-deity; for the temples of Yucatan were undoubtedly dedicated to a deity of that nature. It is not improbable, however, that *Teotl* was really a generic term agreeing in this respect as curiously enough in its form with the Phœnician *Taaut* (*Thoth*).

"The god to whom the temples of Yucatan were really dedicated appears to be *Quetzal-coatl*—by some writers called the feathered serpent, a title belonging to his serpent-father, *Tona-catl-coatl.* This *Quetzal-coatl* was the mysterious stranger who, according to tradition, founded the civilization of Mexico, agreeing thus in his character of a god of wisdom with the Egyptian *Thoth;* reminding us of the resemblance of the name of this deity to that of the Toltecan *Teotl.* But the first part of the name of the Mexican *Quetzal-coatl* no less resembles that borne by the Teutonic deity *Etzel.* *Co-atl* signifies 'the serpent' while *Quetzal* would seem to have reference to the male principle: and thus the idea expressed in the name of the Mexican god is the male principle represented as a serpent. *Quetzal-coatl*, moreover, is said to be an incarnation of *Tonacatl-coatl*, who is the male serpent; his wife being called *Cihua-coatl*, meaning literally the 'woman of the serpent,' or a 'female serpent.'* In

* See *Ancient Symbol-Worship*, pp. 40–41. Mr. Wake then explains this same subject as follows: The serpent was also the symbol of the Egyptian *Kneph*, who resembled the *Sophia* of the Gnostics, the Divine Wisdom. This animal, moreover, was the *Agathodæmon* of the religions of antiquity —the giver of happiness and good fortune. It was in these capacities, rather than as having a phallic significance, that the serpent was associated with the sun-gods, the Chaldean *Bel*, the Grecian *Apollo*, and the Semitic *Seth*. But whence originated the idea of the wisdom of the serpent which led to its connection with the legend of the "fall?" This may, perhaps, be explained by other facts which show also the nature of the wisdom here

the identification then of *Atli* or *Etzel*, who consigns his enemies to the pit of serpents, with the Great Serpent *Ahi* himself, we have a ground of identification of the Teutonic deity with the Mexican serpent-god *Quetzal-coatl.* This view loses none of its probability if the latter is, as Mr. Squier asserts, an incarnation of the serpent-sun, or rather a serpent-incarnation of the Sun-god, since *Ahi* himself is a solar deity.*

"If the comparisons thus made between the Mexican and Teutonic mythologies is correct, the further analogies pointed out by M. Brasseur de Bourbourg may be well founded. Thus the Mexican *Votan* or Odon supposed to be the same as *Quetzal-coatl* may be in reality none other than the Scandinavian *Odin*, *Woden*, or *Wuotan*, who also was a sun-god, and whose name seems to be connected through the root *vad* with the Semitic *ata*, to come, with which there is reason to believe the name of the mythical *Ad* may also be connected."

Having thus adjusted the race-affinities across the Atlantic, Mr. Wake next conducts us among the Polynesian nations. He finds *Ta* to be the name of a "first ancestor," which he considers the same as *At.* But he makes another distinction which ethnologists will be slow to recognize. "Those mythological coinci-

intended. Thus, in the annals of the Mexicans, the first woman, whose name was translated by the old Spanish writers "*the woman of our flesh,*" is always represented as accompanied by a great male serpent. This serpent is the Sun-god *Tonacatl-coatl*, the principal deity of the Mexican pantheon, and the goddess-mother of primitive man is called *Cihua-Cohuatl*, which signifies *wife of the serpent.* According to this legend, which agrees with that of other American tribes, a serpent must have been the father of the human race. This notion can be explained only on the supposition that the serpent was thought to have had at one time a human form. In the Hebrew legend the tempter speaks, and "the old serpent having two feet," of Persian mythology, is none other than the evil spirit Ahriman himself. The fact is that the serpent was only a symbol, or at most an embodiment, of the spirit which it represented, as we see from the belief of certain African and American tribes, which probably preserves the primitive form of this supposition. Serpents are looked upon by these people as embodiments of their departed ancestors, and an analogous notion is entertained by various Hindu tribes. No doubt the noiseless movement and the activity of the serpent, combined with its peculiar gaze and marvellous power of fascination, led to its being viewed as a spirit-embodiment, and hence also as the possessor of wisdom. In the spirit-character ascribed to the serpent, we have the explanation of the association of its worship with human sacrifice noted by Mr. Fergusson—this sacrifice being really connected with the worship of ancestors.

* In the religious symbols used by the Mexicans, Mr. Wake elsewhere remarks, "We have another point of contact with the Asiatic deities. The Sacred Tau (♀) of antiquity has its counterpart on the Mexican monuments. The Mexican symbol perfectly represents the cross-form of the *Tau*, but it is composed of two serpents entwined, somewhat as in the caduceus of Mercury. That the *Tau* itself had such an origin we can well believe, since the name of the letter *Tet* (Θητα) of the Phœnician alphabet specially associated with *Thoth* of whom the *Tau* is a symbol, is that of the God himself, as well as meaning *serpent.*"

dences," he remarks, "are so strongly supported by similarity of customs and linguistic affinities, that there will be no difficulty in classing the Mexicans and kindred American peoples, and even the lighter Polynesians, with the Adamites. This being so, a still broader generalisation than any yet attempted may be made as to the peoples to be included in the Adamic division of the human race. The simplest classification of mankind according to cranial conformation is that of Retzius into dolichocephali or long-heads and brachiocephali or short-heads. The Mexicans and other peoples of the western part of the American continent belong to the latter category, as do also the inhabitants of the area of Asia and Europe. In China and in the southern part of Asia, as well as of Europe, the various peoples are chiefly long-headed; and this is the case with the Hamitic population of Northern Africa. The latter are, however, certainly much mixed with the native African element, which is purely dolichocephalic, exhibiting evidences of its prognathism, and it is far from improbable that originally they were brachiocephalic like the allied peoples of Western Asia. Such also, would I suggest, was the case with the long-headed but orthognathous European and Asiatic peoples we know as Aryans; and with the Chinese and the lighter Polynesians who are now mostly dolichocephalic. Throughout all the regions where these peoples are found there would appear to have been an indigenous long-headed stock, which has more or less nearly absorbed the brachiocephalic element which was introduced long ages ago from the vast regions of Central Asia, and which for the want of a better term may be called *Scythic.* Subject to this qualification it may probably be said that Adamic and short-headed are synonymous terms; and that among the descendants of Father *Ad* may therefore be classed all the peoples who are embraced in the great brachiocephalic division of mankind, or who would have belonged to it if they had not been physically modified by contact with peoples of the more primitive dolichocephalic area."

Hence Mr. Wake finally concludes: "It is difficult, indeed, to say where the descendants of *Ad* are not now to be met with, or where the pre-Adamite is to be found uninfluenced by contact with them."

Professor Agassiz believed that the different human families, like the fauna and flora, were indigenous in particular regions. There is evidently a plurality of human races, and they were doubtless of different age and duration on this globe. Yet they exhibit a far less diversity than the species of animals as they appear on the several continents. The ape tribes have a common tendency toward the human ideal, but even in this respect they display a remarkable diversity from one another. Each tribe approximates humanity from a standing-point peculiarly its own. The uran is very like man in one certain way, but he is not man-like in such a manner as the chimpanzi. The two are formed and developed as if after different models. Mankind could not be evolved from any of them, for the various races of men have one common ideal as human beings. Many of them, to be sure, come so far short of genuine mental and intellectual conditions as to perish without advancing beyond a mere bestial mode of existence. But their form, their mental constitution, so far as it is developed, their very passions and appetites, their peculiar ambitions, show them to be really human beings. Whether they are immortal, whether they possess any rudiment of spirituality in such advanced condition as to eventuate in continued existence with the interior qualities of man cannot now be discussed or any determinate judgment expressed.

Mr. John D. Baldwin, of Worcester, Mass., takes direct issue in several of his works with many of these propositions upon grounds which appear well sustained. He cites the existence of a Malay Empire in the Polynesian Islands, of a duration extending back into prehistoric time. It had not ceased to exist when the Portuguese first voyaged around the Cape of Good Hope. It extended as far as Easter Island and required months for its circumnavigation. "It was maritime and commercial; it had fleets of great ships; and there is evidence that its influence reached most of the Pacific islands." Its metropolis was in the Island of Java; and the remains of Buddhistic temples, and of serpent-worship, are still to be found. But the ancient Peruvians, the Toltecans, and other civilized American nations, differed in type from these Malay populations, and belonged to some other ethnical division.

The character of the aboriginal inhabitants of Hindustan is also in dispute. They have been jumbled together somewhat promiscuously into the Scythic or Turanian class, or rather unclassed tribes of mankind. Several have denominated them negroes, but Sir William Ellis appears to have disposed of this method of shirking the subject. Speaking of the Dravidian races, he says: "Throughout this range I have never observed, during forty years' sojourn, any indication of true Mongolian features. Still less have I seen any signs of Negro blood, save in the instances of imported Africans on the Western Coast." Mr. Baldwin, after propounding the theory that the Cushites or Ethiopians from Arabia had long preceded the Indo-Aryans in Hindustan, adds: "There are strong reasons for believing that the Cushites found the country inhabited by a dark-colored race, similar, perhaps, to the Malays and to the people found on most of the islands of the Indian and Pacific oceans. It was not the policy of the Cushite race to exterminate peoples found in countries which they colonized and occupied. Their policy was to conciliate, civilize and absorb them. The present physical characteristics of the people of India indicate that they pursued this policy in that country."* Prof. Rawlinson adds his testimony: "Recent linguistic discovery tends to show that a Cushite or Ethiopian race did, in the earliest times, extend itself along the shores of the Southern Ocean from Abyssinia to India. The whole peninsula of India was peopled by a race of this character before the inflex of the Aryans; it extended from the Indus along the sea-coast through the modern Beluchistan and Kerman, which was the proper country of the Asiatic Ethiopians. The cities on the northern shores of the Persian Gulf are shown by the brick inscriptions to have belonged to this race; it was dominant in Susiana and Babylonia until overpowered in the one country by Aryan, in the other by Semitic intrusion; it can be traced both by dialect and tradition throughout the whole South coast of the Arabian peninsula, and it still exists in Abyssinia." Again, he treats of "the uniform voice of primitive antiquity which spoke of the Ethiopians as a single race dwelling along the shores of the Southern ocean from India to the Pillars of Hercules."†

Mr. Hyde Clarke would induce us to modify somewhat the views that have been entertained of Asiatic, African, and European ethnology. With a plausibility which is not easy to contend with, taking both history and language for his starting-point, he assumes a racial affinity between the Dravidians of India to the Australians and the Hamites of Northern Africa. The Egyptians and the early inhabitants of Western Europe could not escape the association. Even now there exists good reason for believing that the same dark-skinned race is found on both sides of the Mediterranean. At a period preceding the historic appearance of the Pelasgians, we are now told that Asia Minor and Western Europe were inhabited by races speaking a Dravidian language; anthropologically of a Dravidian type, and historically represented on the monuments of Egypt. Mr. E. R. Hodges also declares that "before the dawn of history overspread Assyria and Mesopotamia, Media and Etruria were the earliest colonists of Britain, Spain, Italy and India." In short, the black Dravidian races are considered as having preceded the whole European family of nations; peopling Asia Minor, Armenia, the country of the Caucasus and Asiatic Ethiopia west of the Indus, as well as France, Spain and the British islands, long before the Semitic and Aryan nations had appeared on the surface of history.

There is a conjecture among scientists that the Asiatic continent once occupied a large part of the Indian ocean. Assuming this to have been the case, we opine that the Dravidian race must be considered as having constituted the population of the submerged territory. The presumed affinity with the Australians would

* J. D. Baldwin: *Prehistoric Nations,* vi. p. 218.

† Rawlinson: *Herodotus,* i. Essay xi. 2, note 8.

warrant this opinion. Nevertheless, we had supposed that the wretched savages of the Andaman islands, Papua, Australia and the mountains of Hindustan, were to be considered as of some race lower than the Dravidian.

Mr. Fergusson, who supports the Turanian hypothesis, is very positive that the Nagas or Serpent-Worshippers of Hindustan could not be "any of the Dravidian races inhabiting the south of India." He says, "It does not appear that the Dravidian races ever were essentially, or to any great extent, serpent-worshippers, or ever were converted to Buddhism."* We are therefore, he concludes, reduced to seeking them among the Dasyus or various original tribes who peopled India before either of these two great dominant races attempted to colonize it. But Ceylon and Burmah, as well as the Vindhaya region and the Punjaub, were peopled by serpent-worshippers who were denominated by their Aryan adversaries, Daisyus and Rakshasas; and serpent-worship was a characteristic of the Ethiopian or Hamitic race. There are Stonehenges in Hindustan as well as in England. The May-pole festival is still in observance there, and the people call their sons Mag or Mac, like the Celts of Scotland and Ireland and the Berbers of Africa.

The pamphlet of Mr. Clarke on *Serpent and Siva Worship*, now republished, appears also to demonstrate a linguistic relation between countries of Africa and America, which had been supposed to be the farthest remote. Names of the most familiar objects in Costa Rica are similar, substantially, to those employed for a like purpose in Africa. Even the "Turanian" countries of China and Japan are not excepted in this connection. It may

* FERGUSSON: *Tree and Serpent-Worship*, Introductory Essay, part II. page 61. Mr. Fergusson also remarks that the Vishnuites are serpent-worshippers. He says: "The Vaishnava religion is derived from a group of faiths in which the serpent always plays an important part. The eldest branch of the family was the Naga worship, pure and simple; out of that arose Buddhism, . . . and on its decline two faiths—at first very similar to one another—rose from its ashes, the Jaina and the Vaishnava. The serpent is almost always found in Jaina temples as an object of veneration, while it appears everywhere in Vaishnava tradition." But elsewhere Mr. Fergusson tells us that, although Buddhism owed its establishment to Naga tribes, yet its supporters repressed the worship of the serpent, elevating tree-worship in its place. According to him, Buddhism was chiefly influential among Naga tribes, and "was little more than a revival of the coarser superstitions of the aboriginal races, purified and refined by the application of Aryan morality, and elevated by doctrines borrowed from the intellectual superiority of the Aryan races." It should not be forgotten that the Vedic religion was not that of all the Aryan tribes of India (See MUIR, *op. cit.*, part ii. p.377, 368–383); and it is by no means improbable that some of them retained a more primitive faith, Buddhism or Rudraism; *i. e.*, Sivaism. To come to a proper conclusion on this important point, it is necessary to consider the real position occupied by Gautama in relation to Brahmanism. Burnouf says that he differed from his adversaries only in the definition he gives of salvation (*du salut*). (*Introduction à l' Histoire du Buddhisme Indien*, p. 155.) Asoka, the great propagandist, was also a worshipper of Siva.

doubtless be carried much farther. India and Japan give to the monkey, the elephant and tapir, the arrow, etc., names almost identical with those used in Africa and Central America.

SIVA, the god-name of India, is far from being as exclusive as we had supposed. We find it in Asia Minor as *Saba* or Sabazius; in Greece as *Seba;* in Central America as *Sibu;* in Africa as *Eshowo.* A snake is *Sapa* in India, *Zebé* or *Kewo* in America, *Hebi* in Japan. Mr. Clarke accumulates evidence of this character from which he brings out the following proposition: "The legend of Siva and Kali is prehistorical, and has survived in Hindu mythology, and been dealt with by a later dominant race." Siva is not mentioned in the *Rig-Veda.* He was no part of the religious system of the Aryan invaders of India, but was a great divinity of the older population. After the establishment of Brahmanism in Hindustan, about twelve centuries ago, he was adopted into the pantheon, together with the the lingham and serpent-symbol. But even now the worshippers of Siva stand aloof from the Vishnuites and devotees of Khrisna. His temples are the oldest in the Dekkan, and he is the god of the sanctuaries excavated in the mountains of Ellora.

Jacob Bryant, following in the track of the ethnology of the tenth chapter of *Genesis,* designated as "Amonians" or children of Ham the dark-skinned populations of India, Persia, Chaldea, Syria, Asia Minor and other countries. Ham, according to Wilford, is an inflection of the name of *Siva.* Mr. Baldwin, though by no means circumscribed to these limits, also denominates these populations, or at least the Arabico-African division, Cushites or Ethiopians. Doubtless a new classification will eventually be adopted by ethnologists, which will leave the Scyths and Mongols out in their native cold. We will be enabled to take our views from a new standing-point.

Signor Gorresio, the translator of the *Ramayana,* believed the people of southern India to be of "Hamitic origin," and cited their use of serpents, dragons and other symbols for proof; also, that the god they prefer to all others, and whom they specially honor in their sacrifices, is "the terrible Rudra or Siva," whom Mr. Baldwin is very certain is a "Cushite divinity," and the one denominated Baal. Dr. Stevenson says: "I observe in Turnour's documents relative to the religion of Ceylon that the whole of that island was overrun with devil and serpent-worship previous to the arrival of Buddha, and I think analogy may lead us to conclude that the same was the case in India before the arrival of the Brahmans."

"The serpent-worship," remarks Mr. Baldwin, "is full of significance. This was a great feature of the religion of the Cushites; but the 'serpent' will convey a very poor notion of its meaning to those who do not understand what it was. The serpent was regarded as a symbol of intelligence, of immortality, of protection against the power of evil spirits, and of a renewal of life or of the healing powers of nature."

The assumed identity of Siva or Bala with the Baal or Moloch-Hercules of the Arabico-Phœnician worship needs only to be placed beyond cavil to give a newer and correcter understanding of history. It shows a unity of idea between the Malayan Empire of the Pacific, the interior population of India, the Ethiopian or Ethiopico-Dravidian nations of Africa, Asia and Europe, that may well excite astonishment. Mr. Baldwin, while insisting that the civilization found in America when it was discovered, had originated there, borrowing nothing from Europe, nevertheless admits a communication with the Mediterranean countries. "Religious symbols," he remarks, "are found in the American rivers which remind us of those of the Phœnicians, such as figures of the serpent, which appear constantly, and the cross, supposed by some to represent the mounting of the magnetic needle, which was among the emblems peculiar to the goddess Astartê. . . . There was sun-worship in America, and the phallic ceremonies existed in some places in the time of Cortez. In Asia, these ceremonies and figures of the serpent were usually associated with sun-worship. Humboldt was sure that these symbols came to America from the Old World."*

The superior evidence of language which has been adduced by Mr. Clarke in these pages should be allowed its full weight, Such actually identical terms to express like ideas, cannot be accidental; and though the past is obscured so that our knowledge does not penetrate its mist and mystery, the facts are very significant and suggestive. Agassiz used to declare this continent to be the really Old World. What, if after all, the Abbe de Bourbourg's conjecture was right, and the Atlantian race actual colonisers of the other hemisphere and apostles of the serpent-religion? We are not prepared to concede the origin of ophiolatry to the inhabitants of India. Yet we are aware that religion is very largely a matter of race; no faith of the same essential character exists in a like form among diverse nations; nor does a people often change the style and form of its worship without retaining the inherent elements very much as they existed before. The various types of Christianity, like those of serpent and Siva worship, are about as numerous as the types of mankind.

* J. D. Baldwin: *Ancient America,* vii. pp. 185, 186.

SERPENT AND SIVA WORSHIP

AND

MYTHOLOGY

IN

CENTRAL AMERICA, AFRICA, AND ASIA.

THESE observations are not intended for a complete treatise, but merely to put on record facts so far as they have been obtained, nor is it intended to draw any absolute conclusion from them, but to indicate materials for inquiry and examination.

In the *Proceedings of the American Philosophical Society* (June and December, 1875, vol. xiv. p. 483) is an elaborate paper on *The Indian Tribes and Languages of Costa Rica*, by Professor W. M. Gabb. This paper, which was read before that Society on August 20, 1875, is most deserving of attention, as well in its anthropological treatment of the subject, as because of the relations of the tribes. It deals with tribes on which the distinguished traveller Von Scherzer obtained little information and on which Bancroft in his great work supplies imperfect matter. Thomas Belt has also visited the country. This is indeed a little book, and, besides the other information, contains copious vocabularies of the Bribri, Cabecar (2), Tiribi, Terraba, and Brunka or Boruka.

This book, having come under my notice, led me to make comparisons with regard to the relations of the languages, which, as usual, proved to be with the Old World.

These Indians are living on both the Atlantic and

Pacific slopes of Costa Rica, in Central America, and are rapidly diminishing and, under Spanish influence, losing their customs and language. A century ago the population was of thousands, now the Changinas are nearly extinct. The Bribris and Cabecars have lessened one-half within twenty years, and now the numbers are:—

Tiribi . . .	103
Uren . . .	604
Bribri . . .	172
Cabecar . . .	128
The Valley . .	219
Altogether .	1,226

Another hundred will cover the Changinas and outlying Cabecars.

It must not be omitted that many of these natives are very light of color and are regarded as whites. One fear, as a consequence of impiety, is being termed black.

This remnant, these tribes of a few scores, are the keepers of knowledge, languages, and legends of the past, which their forefathers brought here thousands of years ago. Some Costa Rica natives still use stone axes set in wooden handles, and those under notice in language belong to the stone age.

The languages collected by Mr. Gabb each possess a vocabulary, which he estimates at between fifteen hundred and two thousand words, a larger number than is vulgarly supposed to be used by savages. The several languages, although differing, are shown by Mr. Gabb to be mutually connected on philological examination, and the further evidence obtained by me confirms this.

As the Bribri is one ground on which the mythological observations rest, it is desirable to enter upon the question of its relations. These could be most readily effected with the African languages of Kœllè's *Polyglotta Africana*, as that work gives more words of culture than the Indian collections of Dr. Hunter, Sir George Campbell, and Colonel Dalton. Indeed, in the present advance of the studies of culture, the Indian vocabularies founded on Brown's basis are by no means calculated to afford results. They contain words of little value in this respect and omit those that are typical. We want much new comparative vocabularies, which will deal less with grammatical points, and provide for names of animals, weapons, tools, etc.

In my comparisons much help was obtained from Mr. Gabb, for in his vocabularies he has carried out a very useful work, in registering the composition and meanings of some of the words. This has been done in some of the Australian vocabularies, but is generally neglected.

It is, however, a process of great importance, and is the foundation for psychological philology, an important branch of anthropology, which is now growing up in strength, but is little appreciated by men of science. Dr. E. B. Tylor, so far as he comprehends philology in his treatises on culture, has collected many useful observations. It is when we learn the thought which governed the application of a word that we know how the human mind operated in the prehistoric epoch, and we are thus building up a history of the human mind. This is indispensable for understanding the beginning and progress of the higher culture when we come, for example, to an epoch so remote as when, in the Mediterranean region, there were at once written monuments of Akkad, of Egypt, and of Khita (Hamath), besides others we know not yet of, and those which must have existed among the Peruvians, the Mayas, and the Mexicans.

Into this school of psychological philology the Germans are entering. Steinthal has expressly dealt with it in his *Philology, its History and Psychology*; and again with Lazarus, in the introduction to their *Journal for Anthropological Psychology and Philology*. Indeed this study has reached the stage of a journal, while in England philology in its higher forms cannot be said to have a society or a journal, and is scarcely tolerated by anthropologists, by whom psychology is little pursued. At the British Association it became a question with naturalists whether philology is a branch of science.

As an evidence of the pursuit of psychological philology in Germany a new example is that afforded by the first volume of the *Coptic Researches* of that distinguished scholar, Dr. Karl Abel, which is almost wholly devoted to the investigation of the words for *Truth* and *Right* in the Egyptian and Coptic languages. In 1859 Dr. Abel began this career by his work on *Languages as the Expression of National Thought*, and in 1871 produced a remarkable treatise on the place of words in Latin construction.

The charm of Professor Max Müller's popular dealings with philology depends on his dealings with these conjoint relations of language and thought in the Aryan languages, and their application in mythology. It is not from want of learning on his part that his labors have by anthropologists been regarded rather as belonging to polite literature than to their science.

One of my objects in my labors on *Prehistoric Comparative Philology* was to illustrate this matter, in direct connection with anthropology, further than Dr. Tylor had done. There will consequently be found there a table of words which are equivalent to each other, and since then my collections have increased. Mr. Gabb's notes enabled me at once to recognise a number of his equivalents as belonging to the prehistoric epoch, and as he gave many which were new, they afforded a good opportunity for testing them with the African.

Thus were used axe, equal to *shoulder-blade;* leaves of a tree for its *hair*, as well as leaf for *tongue;* comb for *hair-scraper;* shirt for *skin;* bowels for *dung-snake;* face for *round*, *sun* and *moon;* handle for *knife*, as the knife's sister; needle for *thorn;* rainbow for *snake;* shield for *shoulder;* river-mouth, as we call it, being *river-tail.*

While examining the equivalents, it appeared the words were sometimes the same in Bribri and in the African, so that a more detailed examination became needful, which showed that *Bribri and its brethren distinctly belonged to the Old World.*

The names of animals show this well:—

Animal names of Costa Rica.

Iguana.
Cabecar, boa.
" ba.

Lizard.
Bute (Afr.), mboa.

Chameleon.
Boko (Afr.), boe.

Frog.
Cabecar, bukwi.
Landoro (Afr.), gbegbe.
Bribri, wem.
Gbese (Afr.), wian.
Kamuku (Afr.), uwama (monkey).
Bribri, koru.
Aku, etc., akere.
Landoro (Afr.), koro (lizard).
Landoro (Afr.), koara (monkey).
Tiribi, orang.
Opanda (Afr.), oranga.
Orongu (Afr.), ironge.
Bribri, koru.

Leopard or Tiger.
Brunka, kura.
Kasm (Afr.), guero.
Bribri, namu.
Nupe (Afr.), nampa.
Bribri, dure.
Nya, Nya, Sandeh (Afr.), nderu (lioness).

Snake.
Bribri, kebe.
Cabecar, kebi.
Kisi (Afr.), kewo.
Tiribi, bgur.
Pika (Afr.), kuredi.
Brunka, tebek.
Landoma (Afr.), abuk.
Bribri, kwa.

Butterfly.
Kano (Afr.), koowa.
Krebo (Afr.), kerakue.
Tiribi, kwong-wo.
Basa (Afr.), kongo.

Bird.
Tiribi, sinwa.
Kumu (Afr.), sin.
Terraba, senowa.
Brunka, dutsut.

Bisfade (Afr.), gunsudu wasudu.

Macaw and Parrot.

Bribri, kukoug.
Cabecar, kukwa.
Bayon, etc. (Afr.), kuakot.
Bribri, pa.
Cabecar, pa.
Bagba (Afr.), pakue.
Cabecar, kwa.
Meto (Afr.), ekuei.
Tiribi, kuskwong.
Ntere (Afr.), nkushu.
Terraba, kishkwong.
Babuma, etc. (Afr.), nkusho.

Bat.

Bribri, dagur.
Aleje (Afr.), kore.

Deer and Goat.

Bribri, siri (also arrow).
Terraba, shuring.
Tene (Afr.), sireme.
Gbese (Afr.), sire.
Kuri (India), siri.

Monkey.

Bribri (C. Amer.), sar.
Cabecar (C. Amer.), sarmatka.
Kuri (India), sara.
Japanese, saru.
Ankaras (Afr.), sirowa.
Basa (Afr.), doe.
Terraba (C. Amer.), do.
Tiribi (C. Amer), duigo.
Aku, etc. (Afr.), edu, edo.
Juku (Afr.), do.
Bribri (C. Amer.), wib.
Terraba (C. Amer.), bib.
Tiribi (C. Amer.), bibgo.
Tiribi (C. Amer.), yaigo.
Tiribi (C. Amer.), duigo.
Kambali (Afr.), wiamo.
Okam (Afr.), iwig.
Mbarike (Afr.), abago.
Biafada (Afr.), gidegwa.
Toronka (Afr.), go.
Toma (Afr.), koe.
Gadaba (India), gusa.
Kol (India), gye.
Garo (India), kouve.
Annam (Asia), khi.
Yerukala (India), kote.
Brunka (C. Amer.), uli.
Eki (Afr.) aile.
Igala (Afr.), ailo (chameleon).
Brunka (C. Amer.), nong.
Dumi (Nepaul), nuksu.
Dhima (India), nhoya.

Elephant—Tapir.

Bribri (C. Amer.), nai.
Cabecar (C. Amer.), nai.
Brunka, nai.
Sobo, etc. (Afr.), eni.
Wolof (Afr.), nyei.
Polo, etc. (Afr.), niwa.
Yerukala (India), ana.
Tamil, anei.
Tiribi, so.
Ngoala (Afr.), eso, so.
Nki (Afr.), eshua.
Aleje (Afr.), esuo.
Naga (India), tsu.
Japanese, zo.

Alligator.

Tiribi (C. Amer.), ku.
Brunka (C. Amer.), kuu.
Bulom (Afr.), kiu.
Timne (Afr.), akui.
Kosi (Afr.), kuiyo.

The name for elephant is enough to mark the connection. As the immigrants had not the elephant they gave his names to his brother the tapir. Thus we find the same names from Central America to Japan. It has been before pointed out by me that there are many names for elephant, and widely spread about, as if the elephant in the prehistoric epoch was better known than in later times. The names for monkey are as widely extended; so we get those for iguana, frog, alligator, bat, deer, and macaw.

The names recognized for objects of culture include arrow, knife, bow, calabash, pot, bed, salt, house, door, skin, cotton, maize, tree, leaf, forest, drum, rope, chair, sand, smoke, coal, dew, rain, night, day.

Central America (Costa Rica).

Arrow.

Bribri, sari.
Tiribi, sure.
Bulom (Afr.), sor.
Timne (Afr.), asor.
Kol (India), sar.
Sanskrit, sara.
Brunka, tunkasa.
Vei (Afr.), tungba.

Nyamba (Afr.), tingowe.
Naga (India), takaba.
Cabecar, ukawu.
Bribri, kabut.
Ondo Aku (Afr.), akofa.
Goali (Afr.), kowi.
Nyamlan (Afr.), ngowe.
Banyun (Afr.), gubande.
Limba (Afr.), kobegare.
Houssa (Afr.), kibia.
Naga (India), takaba.

Bow.

Cabecar, ukaibeta.
Koro (Afr.), buta.
Ntere (Afr.), buta.
Tiwi (Afr.), bada.

Knife.

Tiribi, sugro.
Ashantee (Afr.), sukare.
Cabecar, taberi.
Barba (Afr.), wobaru.
Pulo (Afr.), labi.

Calabash.

Bribri, koku.
Akua (Afr.), koko.
Bola (Afr.), kekanda.
Bribri, kyong.
Vei (Afr.), kungo.
Banyun (Afr.), gukonje.
Diwali (Afr.), ekanga.
Brunka, junkra.
Kamuku (Afr.), sikoara.
Barba (Afr.). karu.
Opanda (Afr.), okodo.
Marawi (Afr.), kika.
Aukaras, kagudu.
Ndob (Afr.), ko.

Pot.

Brunka, kwate.
Landoro (Afr.), kouhwe.
Krebo (Afr.), kowoya.

Bed.

Bribri, akong.
Bamom (Afr.), akon.
Bayon (Afr.), akun.
Njo (Afr.), ekun.
Tiribi, bukru.
Mende (Afr.), buku.

Cabecar, kapugru.
Opanda (Afr.), igberiku.
Gbe (Afr.), gbeko.

Door.

Bribri, shku (ku, mouth).
Toronka (Afr.), ko.
Mende (Afr.), ko.
Aku, etc. (Afr.), eku.
Musu (Nupe) (Afr.), zoko.
Kuru (Afr.), koo.
Yasgua (Afr.), nko.

House.

Bribri, etc., hu.
Tumbuktu (Afr.), hu.
Whidah (Afr.), ho.
Mahi (Afr.), huo.
Ihewe (Afr.), oa.
Boko (Afr.), ua.
Kol (India), oa.

Cotton.

Bribri, sawi.
Ashantee (Afr.), sawa.
Aku (Afr.), owu.

Skin.

Bribri, pa.
Nupese (Afr.), epa, pata.
Kumi (India), pe.
Tiribi, kwota.
Ndob (Afr.), koat, koanyu.
Cabecar, kwo.
Bribri, ikwo.
Murundo (Afr.), ngowo.
Aleje (Afr.), okue.
Tiwi (Afr.), ikuawuro.
" kuare.

Navel.

Tiribi, tuwa.
Bribri, mowu.
Isoama, etc. (Afr.), otuwe.
Bornu (Afr.), dabu.
Bode (Afr.), sabu.
Aku, etc. (Afr.), iwo.

Leaf.

Bribri, ku (also tongue).
Isiele, etc. (Afr.), akukuo.
Gondi (India), aki.
Pulo (Afr.), hako.

Tiwi (Afr.), akoa, ika.
Kra (Afr.), koagi.
Cabecar kargu.
Bribri, karku.
Filham (Afr.), kartoet.
Kaure (Afr.) harugo.

Forest.

Cabecar, karga.
Gbe (Afr.), kurakuli.
Filham (Afr.), karamba.
Bornu (Afr.), karaga.
Akarakura (Afr.), egor.
Tiribi, korgarui.
Bribri, kongyika.
Bode (Afr.), kunu.
Udom (Afr.), akanugbe.

Devil.

Bribri, bi.
Udom, etc. (Afr.), ngbolo.
Nupe (Afr.), abili, beli.

Maize.

Bribri, ikwo.
Cabecar, ikwo.
Nupe (Afr.), kawa.
Opanda (Afr.), agwa.
Eafen (Afr.), nkui.
Mbe (Afr.), ekui.
Brunka, kup.
Kupa (Afr.), akaba.
Landoma (Afr.), kebabu.

Tree.

Bribri, kar.
Tiribi, kor.
Toma, etc. (Afr.), guru.
Bambara (Afr.), koroma.

Drum.

Bribri, sebak.
Pulo (Afr.), baga.
Konguan (Afr.), baka.

Rope.

Bribri, tsa.
Noojin (Afr.), sei.
Pika (Afr.), tsoli.
Juku (Afr.), dsa.
Bribri, duki.
Okuloma (Afr.), digi.
Ndob (Afr.), ndek, ndik.

Chair.
Bribri, kru.
Aro (Afr.), nkoro.
Gajaga (Afr.), korondamo.

Sand.
Bribri, tsoug.
Cabecar, ksoug.
Basa (Afr.), atsikono.
Nupe (Afr.), jikana.
Bribri, chika.
Kasauj (Afr.), kisegelo.
Tiribi, erasho.
Aku, etc. (Afr.), irai.

Smoke.
Tiribi, nyo.
Guresa (Afr.), nyusha.
Yula (Afr.), nyue.
Nupe (Afr.), nawu, nau.
Legba (Afr.), nyos.
Bribri, shkono.
Yala (Afr.), noala.
Basa (Afr.), inshiko.

Coal.
Cabecar, jikowo.
Ebe (Nupe) (Afr.), jikara.
Cabecar, jikowa.
Abaja (Afr.), ujekolono.

Dew.
Cabecar, moriu.
Gureşha (Afr.), marulam.
Bribri, moweli.
Mose (Afr.), worodo.
Tiribi, tomboria.
Mandengo, etc. (Afr.), buru.
Adampe (Afr.), debuloku.

Rain.
Tiribo, shunyo.
Toronka (Afr.), sanyiyi.
Brunka, jo.
Mandengo, etc. (Afr.), sanjo.
Ujo (Afr.), osuo.
Goali (Nupe) (Afr.), sheogo.
Bribri, kawni.
Cabecar, kani.
Jelana (Afr.), keah.
Limba (Afr.), koyon.

Night.
Tiribi, shke.
Goali (Nupe) (Afr.), suko.
Ngola (Afr.), osoko.
Deoria Chutia (Asia), sakokoi.

Day.
Cabecar, kanyina.
Soso (Afr.), yanyina.
Brunka, daboi.
Nhalemoi (Afr.), boisale.

Salt.
Bribri, deje.
Undaza (Afr.), leje.
Nupe (Afr.), esa.
Adampe (Afr.), eje.

God.
Bribri, sibu.
Terraba, zubo.
Udom, etc. (Afr.), eshowo.
Nupe, etc. (Afr.), soko.
Mbofia (Afr.), juku.
Kabenda, etc. (Afr.), nzambi.
Ndob (Afr.), nzob.

These comparisons brought me to the names for *god* and *devil*. As SIBU, the name for God in Central America, was represented in Africa, it was consequently prehistoric, and afforded an early, if not a primary, fact in mythology. This investigation was consequently pursued, and the following table will exhibit the main facts.

God.
Ekamtulufu (Afr.), eshowo.
Udom (Afr.), eshowo.
Ntere (Afr.), njami.
Mutsaya (Afr.), ndzama.
Nyamba (Afr.), ntsuma.
Kasanj, etc. (Afr.), nsambi.
Babuma, etc. (Afr.), njambi.
Kabenda, etc. (Afr.), nzambi.
Nyombe (Afr.), ndzambi.
Nupe, etc. (Afr.), soko.
Eshitako (Afr.), soko.
Goali (Afr.), siogoli.
Musu (Afr.), seangoi.
Isoama, etc. (Afr.), juku.
Legba, etc. (Afr.), esho.
Mende (Afr.), ngewo.
Melon, etc. (Afr.), [nyama.]
Bribri (C. Amer.), sibu.
Cabecar (C. Amer.), sibu.
Tiribi (C. Amer.), zibo.
Terraba (C. Amer.), zubo.
Brunka (C. Amer.), siboh.
Phrygia (Asia), saba (sabazios).
India (Asia), siva, shiva.
Greece (Europe), seba, (worship.)
India (Asia), kali.

Devil.
Sarar, usawe.
Soso, masibo.
Okuloma, sibiribo.
Kasanj, nsumbi.
Undaza, ujumbi.
Marawa, joka.
Pangela, namatubia.
Aro (Afr.), iguakala.
Boko (Afr.), kali.

Phallus.
Bribri, kibiwo.

Snake.

Fulup, etc., siweba.
Tene, masiwo.
Dewoi, zebê, zewê.
Gajaga, samako.
Muntu, lidsoga.
Marawi, njoka.
Kisi, kewo.
Aku, ejo.
Undaza, tadi.
Mutsaya, tadê.
Bribri, kibi.
Cabecar, kebi.
Brunka, tebek.
Sak (India), kapu.
Tharu (India), sapa.
Pakhya (India), sapa.
Chentsu (India), sap.
Kooch (India), samp.
Japan, hebi.
Vayu (India), habu.
Java, sawer.
Gondi, etc. (India), todas.
Basque (Europe), sugê.
Landoro, etc. (Afr.), kali.

Idol.

Krebo, kusewe.
" sewe.
Vei, nowe.
Igala, odsibo.
Kiamba, zewa.
Abaja, ishiafa.
Opanda, odsibo.
Yala, ejibe (greegree).
Sobo, sebo (sacrifice).
Egbir (sacrifice), esewo.
Lubulo (sacrifice), ndzumbi.
Sobo, ejo.
Abandi, ngafu.

Heaven, Sky.

Ekamtulufu, nebo.
Mbofon, sowo-nebo.
Udom, lebo.
Aleje; lebue.
Nyombe, ndzambi.
Lubulo, koandzambi.
Isoama, juko.
Kra, juku.
[Tibetan, nam.]
Russian, nebo.

Navel, Belly.

Wun, nawo.
Musu, nubo.
Aleje, nefo.
Kamuku, liuwu.
Yala, lepu.
Gajaga, sumpo.
Kasanj, mujimbi.
Bode, sabu.
Tiwi, ijombo.
Muntu, masaku.
Baghrmi, jiwili.
Kandin, jibia.
Houssa, jibia.
Juku, juko.
Houssa (belly), jiki.
Kandin (belly), jiki.
" tedis.
Isoama, otuwe.
Abaja, otubo.
Bribri, mowo.
Tiribi, tuwa.
" (belly), bowo.
Brunka, tuwong.
Soso (Afr.), kuli.
Abandi (Afr.), ngoli.

Fish.

Kisi, suwa.
Fulup, siwol.
Kisi, siwo.
Dewoi, zemi.
Gurma, jamu.
Goali, siowo.
Banyun, jokorot.
Mimboma, zimpfu.
Musentandu, zimbizi.
Muntu, usomba.
Marawi, tsomba.
Bribri, nima.
Japanese, siwo.
Tamil (India), chepa.
Finnish, kala.

Sibu or Sowo being the god, the name was of course found for spirit or devil, such degradations of an older god being a leading fact in mythology. It was also found under the same conditions as *idol*, *sacrifice*, and *greegree.* The conformity of *god* and *sky* is a mythological fact well known in Aryan mythology, and indeed it is the basis of the common school of weather-mythology, in which the phenomena of the mythologies of the whole world is dealt with in a favorite method. It is, however, a prehistoric fact, predominating Aryan and later operations, and it applies to Sibu.

In searching for the meaning of the name *Sibu*, reasons led me to seek in that for *navel*, and it will be found fully represented. Navel and belly words are intermixed. The bowel, however, takes the name of a snake, and this led me to look for snake as an equivalent.*

* THEODORET : *Hæret. Fabul.* i. 13. *De Ophiacis.* "The serpent imitating the winding position of the intestines exhibits the wisdom of the life-producer ; therefore they adore the serpent."

Snake is further equivalent to fish.* The rainbow is also a snake in Bribri. Thus we have a whole apparatus for the mythology of serpent-worship and the powers of nature.

On examining eastward for *sibo*, or *sowo*, and *nebo*, many indications present themselves. Nebo or Nabo is the name of a Chaldean god (says Dr. W. Smith), a well-known deity of the Babylonians and Assyrians. In Babylonia Nebo held a prominent place from an early time, and his name forms part of the names of many kings, as Nebuchadnezzar. It is extraordinary that the population of Nebaioth, in Arabia, is found closely connected with the Sabæans.

The question arises whether the rock-monument of Niobê on Mount Sipylus, near Magnesia and Smyrna, may not have been a Nebo. The ancient writers dispute whether it was a man or a woman. The name *Sipulus*, I thought, was Suburu, (Akkad,) a statue (*Prehistoric Comparative Philology*), but it may also relate to *sibu*. Every trace of speculation is worth following. Nebo was a mountain-name in Palestine.

Seba, in Greek, signifies worship, adoration, veneration, and is worthy of notice as indicating a possible relation to the ancient worship, and with which the term *Sabazios* may be connected.

There was an Ethiopian god, Assabinus, that is, Assabi or Sabi. Seb, Seb-ra, or Sobok, was a god of the Egyptians, equivalent to Kronos.

Saba was a very old Arabian king.†

One of the Hebrew names of God is צבאות, *Tsebaoth* or *Sebaoth*. This is commonly translated *Lord of hosts* or armies, but it is more possibly *Seba*. It is to be observed that there are doubts among the Talmudists whether Sebaoth is properly a Hebrew name of God, and whether it is not profane. Turning it to Zeus and Dyaus, a new conjecture for their origin presents itself.

In Smith's and the other dictionaries, is to be found *Sabasius* or *Sabazios*, and the materials are most confused. He was made into Jupiter Sabazios or Dionusus Sabazios (Bacchus). ‡ Re-constructing the materials, we find Saba,

* The words also cover the phallus.

† Rev. Prof. Campbell: *The Hivites*, p. 28.

‡ Strabo, the geographer, stated that the exclamations originated in the east, which were made at the Sabazian festival: "Evoè! Sabai! Bacchi!

an old god of Phrygia, whose worship extended over Asia and Greece. He was torn by the Titans into seven pieces. Serpents figured largely in the initiations, midnight mysteries, and processions. A golden serpent was dropped into the bosom of the initiate, falling out of the bottom of the frock. Mixed up in time with the later mythology, it was a religion of the populace, and by the more scientific was found to belong to Zeus and Dionusus. Demosthenes looked upon it as disreputable.

With these stepping-stones we come to India, and we find Siva as a member of the Hindu Trimurti under most peculiar circumstances. He is, in most cases, co-equal with Brahma and Vishnu, and his powers and properties are intermingled with theirs. His wife is Kali. They hold their own to this day as popular gods.

Applying our material to deal with Siva or Shiva and Kali, we find not only the former name but the latter in Africa. The connections are those of Siva. Many of the Hindu gods are decorated with snakes, for such is the inheritance of serpent-worship, but Siva is more particularly so provided.

There are two Hindu legends of the Creation, but that most popularly depicted represents Vishnu sleeping on a serpent, Ananta, on the face of the waters, after the annihilation of a former Creation. From his navel springs a long stem ending in a lotus, and from this Brahma is born, who produces Siva. The three are, however, brothers born together. Thus the belly is the seat of creation, and from the navel proceeds the stem, which must be assimilated to the snake of the bowel. We have the conformity in this main Siva-legend of the god, his wife, of the navel, and the snake. In the present state of Siva-worship we have the increments of various ages and of various races, corresponding to those which in a shorter period affected Sabazios in Phrygia and Greece. *We are justified in regarding Siva and Kali as a prehistoric legend, which has survived in Hindu mythology and been dealt with by a later dominant race.*

Turning back to Central America, we find in the scanty gleanings of Mr. Gabb many things very suggestive. Sibu is the one god, but he has twenty names. The people were very indignant at the proposition that

Hues! Attes! Hues!" Doctor Waite has rendered them into a Sanskrit expression: *Aho! Siva, Isa; Ad'hisa; Adye Seva!*—Hail, O Siva! Lord, Supreme Lord, Hail to the first-existing.

there was more than one god. A distinct line is drawn between Sibu and the numerous local or individual spirits, demons, or devils and ghosts of the dead. So, too, Capt. Hay says that in Akem, in the corresponding district in West Africa, the god is one god. This is a very remarkable feature corresponding to the cardinal doctrine of Hindu mythology, and it is suggestive of a widely-spread doctrine in the early prehistoric epochs. The divinity is one, but he is the spirit of all nature in every form, and in every development of the operations of the natural world. Each man was a manifestation of him.

The staff of the priests is gathered with care and devotion from a mystic timber, because it is guarded by a venomous snake. A circumstance particularly noticed by Mr. Gabb is that the songs of the priests are in a peculiar language, and although most anxious to obtain information on this head, he was most unfortunately prevented.

A curious fact must not be omitted, although not immediately relevant. In Santo Domingo there are no venomous reptiles; but, says Mr. Gabb, a poisonous plant is called *kibe*, which is the same as the Bribri *kebe*, snake. Shiva or Shivatt was the Mexican god of war.

In the table of Sibu-names, a few words belonging to the series are introduced, but, as a general principle, the names of the great local god of African tribes conform with navel and snake, like *sibu*.

With regard to the tree, it is good to note some points which illustrate its worship and the doctrine of Dryads.

With us we talk of the arms of a tree, but in the complete notion of a tree in Africa and Central America there is the trunk, the head, the arms. The leaves figure as fingers or as tongues. In the latter relation we have the idea of the Dryads speaking. The roots, however, have their distinct meaning. In Africa they are toes (see *table*); in Central America the buttock of the tree. Thus the tree is a complete being on the model of a man, and animation is only a stage forward.

So as to the river. We are familiar with its heads and arms, and in the prehistoric epoch it had its heads and arms; but what we call mouths are in Bribri the buttock or rump. In the case of the river it was most easy to anticipate its possession of a life, and the stage of its worship was a sequence to be looked for.

	Root.	*Toe.*
Gbe (Afr.)	gbire	bie-gbure, G. gbere, Nupe
Adampe	atike	dide, A.
Kasm	nade	nanina, K.
Sobo	owuse	isiawo, S.
Oloma	ugo	ikanena, O.
Gura	kurugulo	kieroguro, G.
Boko	gesane	kisa, B.
Konguan	nkanok	henuraka, K. ekinafien, Mbarike.
Pajade (Afr.)	pukade	pukan, Bola (Afr.), etc.
Soso (Afr.)	sankei	senkonne, Mandingo.
Tene (Afr.)	baride	berai, Gbando.
Soso (fing.) (Afr.)	bile	bulo, Mandingo (Afr.)
Koama (Afr.)	nakel	nika, Kiamba (Afr.)
Isoama (Afr.)	oboroko	ngbaroga, Ishieli (Afr.)
Yorubo	egbogi	agbalogba, Abaji.
Undaza	moakanga	moaku, Ndobu.

Toe is of course in many cases the same as finger.

The seat of Sibu is in the sky, in the zenith, that is, in the navel of the day, and its sphere or belly.

In Bribri, the rainbow is a snake of the sky for the day, and we may expect to find that the milky way is the snake of the night. So we witness the rainbow serving as a road for gods and their messengers, and again Watling-street or the milky way serving as their road.

As a further instance of the light which may be obtained from African sources, to illustrate the origin of mythology, a more direct example than that of Sabazios may be taken.

The mythology of Greece and Asia Minor is usually mixed together, and treated as of one type, and hence there is a difficulty in ascertaining its true relations. That of Thebes, in Bœotia, if separated from the other centres, affords materials useful for comparison.

The names of the kings of Thebes, their wives and children, form a remarkable series.

	Children.	
Cadmus = Hermionê.	Ino. Echion.	Agavê.
Athamas = Nephelê.	Phryxus.	Hellê.
" = Ino.	Learchus.	Melikertes. (Palæmon.)
Amphion = Niobê		
Echion = Agavê.	Pentheus.	

In the Caucasus we have

Prometheus.	Deucalion.	
Epimedes [Epimetheus] = Pandora.		Pyrrha.

In Phœnicia we have

Poseidôn = Libya.		Agenor.	Belus.

Elsewhere we have

Herakles = Hebê.	

A similarity of names is shown in

Adam = Khaveh.		Cain.	Abel.

The incidents of the Theban and allied legends have many points of similarity. The men are founders; there is a creation (Cadmus, Prometheus); a woman is created (Pandora); the woman is the cause of evil (Ino, Pandora, Agavê); nakedness and dress are referred to (Hebê, Pandora); there is a contest with serpents (Cadmus); they are subjected to exile; the son is killed and the children are unfortunate (Palæmon, and children of Niobê, Cadmus, Echion, and Libya).

In Africa the names of the women of these legends are found in some allied roots.

חוה	Khaveh, Hebê	Ewa (Ira)	Rib	Egba.
חוה	Khaveh, Agavê	Kafef	"	Filham.
		Gafe	"	Bodê.
Αγαυη	Agavê	Eguha	"	Yoruba, etc.
		Eguaya	"	Ota.
		Agelag	"	Abaja.
חוה	Khaveh	Efê	"	Bini, etc.
Ἡβη	Hebê	Aba	"	Kupa, etc.

Nephelê, Pandora, Niobê, and Ino, can also be distinguished. They are also names for sisters or women. Abel (Mbale) and Cain (Kana) are names given to elder and younger brothers.

Rib is the root, which is equivalent to side,* and thereby to brother and sister. So, too, in Akkad, *bab* signifies side, rib, and mother. Thus it is easy to conceive Evê, or Agavê, being treated as the rib or side. This word

* The Hebrew word in *Genesis* ii. 21, 22, is צלע *tzalo,* and is defined by Parkhurst, a *rib,* a *side,* or *lateral extremity* (*Exodus* xxv. 12; *II. Samuel* xvi. 13; *Job* xviii. 12), a *side-room.* The verb צלע *tzalo* signifies to go *sideways,* as at the Baalic or Amazonian chorus or circle-dance of the Mysteries—also to *halt* or *limp.* The noun צלם *tzalam* (*Genesis* i. 26 and v. 3, *et passim*), signifies a *form, likeness, image, apparition, appearance, fantasy, shadow.* It is possible that the word rendered *rib* ought to have been understood as *image, likeness, copy, simulacrum.* The ancient practice of the Bible-writers and old mythologists of using puns and words of like sound for purposes of symbology is thus fully illustrated.—A. W.

Gafa, or Gaba is also a negative, and in some instances signified night. Thus a community of idea of night or sleep, rib, and death and evil, is provided in the words as the material for legend, and with the two words for elder and younger brother, a community of legend was prefigured in prehistoric times which could be distributed in the various regions of the earth.

THE

ORIGIN OF SERPENT-WORSHIP.

BY C. STANILAND WAKE, M.A.I.

THE subject proposed to be discussed in the present paper is one of the most fascinating that can engage the attention of anthropologists. It is remarkable, however, that although so much has been written in relation to it, we are still almost in the dark as to the origin of the superstition in question. The student of mythology knows that certain ideas were associated by the peoples of antiquity with the serpent, and that it was the favorite symbol of particular deities; but why that animal rather than any other was chosen for the purpose is yet uncertain. The facts being well known, however, I shall dwell on them only so far as may be necessary to support the conclusions based upon them.

We are indebted to Mr. Fergusson* for bringing together a large array of facts, showing the extraordinary range which serpent-worship had among ancient nations, It is true that he supposes it not to have been adopted by any nation belonging to the Semitic or Aryan stock; the serpent-worship of India and Greece originating, as he believes, with older peoples. However this may be, the superstition was certainly not unknown to either Aryans or Semites. The brasen serpent of the Hebrew *Exodus*

* JAMES FERGUSSON, D.C.L., F.R.S., etc.: *Tree and Serpent-Worship; or Illustrations of Mythology and Art in India in the First and Fourth Centuries after Christ.* 1868.

was destroyed in the reign of Hezekiah, owing to the idolatry to which it gave rise. In the mythology of the Chaldeans, from whom the Assyrians seem to have sprung, the serpent occupied a most important position. Among the allied Phœnicians and Egyptians, it was one of the most divine symbols. In Greece, Hercules was said "to have been the progenitor of the whole race of serpent-worshipping Scythians, through his intercourse with the serpent Echidna"; and when Minerva planted the sacred olive on the Acropolis of Athens, she placed it under the care of the serpent-deity Erichthonios. As to the Latins, Mr. Fergusson remarks that "Ovid's *Metamorphoses* are full of passages referring to the important part which the serpent performed in all the traditions of classic mythology." The superstitions connected with that animal are supposed not to have existed among the ancient Gauls and Germans; but this is extremely improbable, considering that it appears to have been known to the British Celts and to the Gothic inhabitants of Scandinavia. In Eastern Europe there is no doubt that the serpent-superstition was anciently prevalent; and Mr. Fergusson refers to evidence proving that "both trees and serpents were worshipped by the peasantry in Esthonia and Finland within the limits of the present century, and even with all the characteristics possessed by the old faith when we first become acquainted with it."

The serpent entered largely into the mythology of the ancient Persians, as it does into that of the Hindus. In India it is associated with both Sivaism and Vishnuism, although its actual worship perhaps belonged rather to the aboriginal tribes, among whom Buddhism is thought by recent writers to have originated. The modern home of the superstition, however, is western Africa, where the serpent is not merely considered sacred, but is actually worshipped as divine. On the other side of the Indian Ocean traces of the same superstition are met with among the peoples of the Indian islands and of Polynesia, and also in China. The evidences of serpent-worship on the American continent have long engaged the attention of archæologists, who have found it to be almost universal, under one form or another, among the aboriginal tribes. That animal was sculptured on the temples of Mexico and Peru, and its form is said by Mr. Squier to be of frequent occurrence among the mounds of Wisconsin. The most remarkable of the symbolic earthworks of North America is the great serpent-mound of Adams county, Ohio, the convolutions of which extend to a length of 1000 feet. At the Edinburgh meeting of the British Association, in 1871, Mr. Phené gave an account of his discovery in Argyllshire of a similar mound several hundred feet long, and about fifteen feet high by thirty feet broad, tapering gradually to the tail, the head being surmounted by a circular cairn, which he supposes to answer to the solar disk above the head of the Egyptian *uræus*, the position of which, with head erect, answers to the form of the Oban serpent-mound. This discovery is of great interest, and its author is probably justified in assuming that the mound was connected with serpent-worship. I may remark, in evidence of the existence of such structures in other parts of the old world, that the hero of one of the *Yaçnas* of the *Zend-Avesta* is made to rest on what he thinks is a bank, but which he finds to be a great green snake, doubtless a serpent-mound.* Another ancient reference to these structures is made by Iphicrates, who, according to Bryant, "related that in Mauritania there were dragons of such extent that grass grew upon their backs."

Let us now see what ideas have been associated with the serpent by various peoples. Mr Fergusson mentions the curious fact that "the chief characteristic of the serpents throughout the East in all ages seems to have been their power over the wind and rain." According to Colonel Meadows Taylor, in the Indian Dekkan, at the present day, offerings are made to the village divinities (of whom the nâg, or snake, is always one) at springtime and harvest for rain or fine weather, and also in time of cholera or other diseases or pestilence. So, among the Chinese, the dragon is regarded as the giver of rain, and in time of drought offerings are made to it. In the spring and fall of the year it is one of the objects worshipped, by command of the Emperor, by certain mandarins. The Chinese notion of the serpent or dragon dwelling above the clouds in spring to give rain reminds us of the Aryan myth of Vritra, or Ahi, the throttling snake, or dragon with three heads, who hides away the rain-clouds, but who is slain by Indra, the beneficent giver of rain. "Whenever," says Mr. Cox, "the rain is shut up in the clouds, the dark power is in revolt against Dyaus and Indra. In the rumblings of the thunder, while the

* *Yaçna*, ix. 33–39.

drought still sucks out the life of the earth, are heard the mutterings of their hateful enemy. In the lightning flashes which precede the outburst of the pent-up waters are seen the irresistible spears of the god, who is attacking the throttling serpent in his den; and in the serene heaven which shone out when the deluging clouds are passed away, men beheld the face of the mighty deity who was their friend." Mr Cox elsewhere remarks that Vritra, "the enemy of Indra, reäppears in all the dragons, snakes, or worms slain by all the heroes of Aryan mythology."

Whether the Great Serpent be the giver or the storer of rain, the Aryans, like all eastern peoples, suppose it to have power over the clouds. This, however, is only one of its attributes. It is thought to have power over the wind as well as the rain, and this also is confirmed by reference to Aryan mythology. Mr. Cox has well shown that Hermes is "the air in motion, or wind, varying in degree from the soft breath of a summer breeze to the rage of the growing hurricane." In these more violent moods he is represented by the Maruts, the "crushers" or "grinders," who are also the children of Rudra, the "Father of the Winds," and himself the "wielder of the thunderbolt" and the "mightiest of the mighty." Rudra is also "the robber, the cheat, the deceiver, the master-thief," and in this character both he and Hermes agree with the cloud-thief Vritra.

Notwithstanding the fact that in the *Mahâbharâta*, Rudra, like Hercules, is described as the "destroyer of serpents," he is in the same poem identified with Mahadeva, and hence he is evidently the same as Siva, who has the title of King of Serpents. The primitive character of Siva, as the Vedic Rudra, is now almost lost, but the identity of the two deities may be supported by reference to an incident related in the myth of Hermes and Apollo. It is said that, in return for the sweet-sounding lyre, Apollo gave to Hermes the magical "three-leafed rod of wealth and happiness." Sometimes this rod was entwined with serpents instead of fillets, and there is no difficulty in recognising in it the well-known emblem of Siva, which also is sometimes encircled by serpents. It can be shown that the Hindu deity is a form of Kronos or Saturn, one of the Semitic names for whom was Set or Seth. It was the serpent-symbol of this God * which

* Theodoret did not distinguish between an Egyptian sect called *Sethians* and the Gnostic *Ophites* or serpent-worshippers.

was said to have been elevated in the wilderness for the healing of the people bitten by serpents, and curiously enough Rudra (Siva) was called not only the *bountiful*, the *strong*, but the *healer*. The later Egyptian title of the god Set was Typhon, of whom Mr. Bréal says that "Typhon is the monster who obscures the heaven, a sort of Greek Vritra." The myth of Indra and Vritra is reproduced in Latin mythology as that of Hercules and Căcus. Căcus also is analogous to Typhon, and as the former is supposed to have taken his name from, or given it to, a certain wind which had the power of clothing itself with clouds, so the latter bore the same name as a very destructive wind which was much dreaded by the Phœnicians and Egyptians. Moreover, the name Typhon was given by the Egyptians to anything tempestuous, and hence to the ocean; and in Hebrew the allied word "Suph" denotes a "whirlwind." There is another point of contact, however, between Siva and the god Set or Typhon, who was known to the Egyptians also as the serpent Aphôphis, or the giant. An ancient writer states that one of the names of El, or Kronos, was Typhon; and the serpent and pillar symbols of the Phœnician deity confirm the identification between Set or Saturn, and the Siva of the Hindu pantheon.

One of the leading ideas connected with the serpent was, as we have seen, its power over the rain; but another equally influential was its connection with health. Mr. Fergusson remarks that "when we first meet with serpent-worship, either in the wilderness of Sinai, the groves of Epidaurus, or in the Sarmatian huts, the serpent is always the Agathodæmon, the bringer of health and good fortune." * The Agathodæmon, which in ancient Egypt presided over the affairs of men as the guardian spirit of their houses,† was the Asp of Ranno, the snake-headed goddess who is represented as nursing the young princes. That the idea of health was intimately associated with the serpent is shown by the crown formed of the asp, or sacred *Thermuthis*, having been given particularly to Isis, a goddess of life and healing. It was also the sym-

* The heavenly serpent, *Danh*, of the Dahomans, is said by Captain Burton to be the god of wealth. "His earthly representative is esteemed the supreme bliss and general good." The Slavonian Morlacchi still consider that the sight of a snake crossing the road is an omen of good fortune. —WILKINSON: *Dalmatia and Montenegro*, vol. ii. p. 160.

† Mr. Lane states that each quarter of Cairo is supposed to have its guardian genius, or agathodæmon, in the form of a serpent.—Vol. i. p. 289.

bol of other deities with the like attributes. Thus on papyri it encircles the figure of Harpocrates, who was identified with the serpent-god Æsculapius; while not only was a great serpent kept alive in the temple of Serapis, but on later monuments this deity is represented by a great serpent, with or without a human head. Sanchoniathon says of that animal: "It is long-lived, and has the quality not only of putting off its old age and assuming a second youth, but of receiving at the same time an augmentation of its size and strength." The serpent, therefore, was a fit emblem of Rudra "the healer"; and the gift which Apollo presented to Mercury could be entwined by no more appropriate object that the animal which was supposed to be able to give the health without which even Mercury's magic staff could not confer wealth and happiness. It is remarkable that a Moslem saint of Upper Egypt is still thought to appear under the form of a serpent, and to cure the diseases which afflict the pilgrims to his shrine.

Ramahavaly, one of the four national idols of the Madacasses, bears a curious analogy to the serpent-gods of wisdom and healing. One of his titles is *Rabiby*, signifying "animal," and denoting "the god of beasts"; and his emissaries are the serpents which abide in Madagascar, and are looked upon with superstitious fear by the inhabitants. Ramahavaly is, moreover, regarded as the Physician of Imerina, and is thought to preserve from, or expel, epidemic diseases. Mr. Ellis says that he is sometimes described "as god, sacred, powerful, and almighty; who kills and makes alive; who heals the sick, and prevents diseases and pestilence; who can cause thunder and lightning to strike their victims or prevent their fatality; can cause rain in abundance when wanted, or can withhold it so as to ruin the crops of rice. He is also celebrated for his knowledge of the past and future, and for his capacity of discovering whatever is hidden or concealed."

It is probable that the association with the serpent of the idea of healing arose from the still earlier recognition of that animal as a symbol of life. I have already referred to the representations in the Egyptian temples of the young princes being nursed by a woman having the head of an asp. It is interesting to find that in India at the present day serpent-worship is expressly resorted to on behalf of children, and "the first hair of a child which is shaved off when it has passed teething and other infantine ailments is frequently dedicated to a serpent." This animal in both cases is treated as the guardian of life, and therefore the crown given to Egyptian sovereigns and divinities was very properly formed of the asp of Rânno. Another snake-headed Egyptian goddess has the name *Hih* or *Hoh*, and Sir Gardner Wilkinson mentions that the Coptic word *Hof* signifies the viper, analogous to the *hye* of the Arabs. The Arabic word *hiya*, indeed, means both life and a serpent. This connection is supported by the association, already pointed out, between the serpent and the gods of the life-giving wind, and by the fact that these also possess the pillar-symbol of life. This belongs as well to Siva the destroyer, the preserver, and the creator, as to Set or Saturn, to Thoth-Hermes, and El or Kronos. Both the serpent and the pillar were assigned also to many of the personifications of the sun, the deified source of earthly life. Probably the well-known figure representing the serpent with its tail in its mouth, was intended to symbolize endless life rather than eternity; an idea which does not appear to have been associated with that animal by the Egyptians. Agreeably with this view, Hor-Apollo affirms that Kneph-Agathodæmon denoted immortality.

One of the best-known attributes of the serpent is WISDOM. The Hebrew tradition of the fall speaks of that animal as the most subtile of the beasts of the field; and the founder of Christianity tells his disciples to be as wise as serpents, though as harmless as doves. Among the ancients the serpent was consulted as an oracle, and Maury points out that it played an important part in the life of several celebrated Greek diviners in connection with the knowledge of the language of birds, which many of the ancients believed to be the souls of the dead. The serpent was associated with Apollo and Athené, the Grecian deities of wisdom, as well as with the Egyptian Kneph,* the ram-headed god from whom the Gnostics are sometimes said to have derived their idea of the *Sophia*. This personification of divine wisdom is undoubtedly represented on Gnostic gems under the form of the serpent. In Hindoo mythology there is the same association between that animal and the

* Warburton supposes that the worship of the One God Kneph was changed into that of the dragon or winged-serpent Knuphis.

idea of wisdom. Siva, as Sambhu, is the patron of the Brâhmanic order, and, as shown by his being three-eyed, is essentially a god possessing high intellectual attributes. Vishnu also is a god of wisdom, but of the somewhat lower type which is distinctive of the worshippers of truth under its feminine aspect. The connection between wisdom and the serpent is best seen, however, in the Hindu legends as to the Nagas. Mr. Fergusson remarks that "the Naga appears everywhere in Vaishnava tradition. There is no more common representation of Vishnu* than as reposing on the Sesha, the celestial seven-headed snake, contemplating the creation of the world. It was by his assistance that the ocean was churned and Amrita produced. He everywhere spreads his protecting hood over the god or his avatars; and in all instances it is the seven-headed heavenly Naga, not the earthly cobra of Siva." The former animal, no doubt, is especially symbolical of wisdom, and it is probably owing to his intellectual attributes rather than to his destructive or creative power that Siva is sometimes styled the King of Serpents. The *Upanishads* refer to the science of serpents, by which is meant the wisdom of the mysterious Nagas who, according to Buddhistic legend, reside under Mount Méru, and in the waters of the terrestial world. One of the sacred books of the Tibetan Buddhists is fabled to have been received from the Nagas, who, says Schlagentweit, are "fabulous creatures of the nature of serpents, who occupy a place among the beings superior to man, and are regarded as protectors of the law of Buddha. To these spiritual beings Sâkya-muni is said to have taught a more philosophical religious system than to men, who were not sufficiently advanced to understand it at the time of his appearance." So far as this has any historical basis, it can mean only that Gautama taught his most sacred doctrines to the Nagas, or aboriginal serpent-worshippers, who were the first to accept his teaching, and whose religious ideas had probably much in common with those of Gautama himself. Mr. Fergusson refers to the fact that a king of the Naga race was reigning in Magadha when Buddha was born in 623 B.C.; and he adds that the dissemination of his religion "is wholly due to the accident of its having been adopted by the low-caste kings of Magadha, and to its having been elevated by one of them to the rank of the religion of

* Vishnu is often identified with Kneph.

the state." It would appear, indeed, that according to a Hindu legend, Gautama himself had a serpent-lineage.

The "serpent-science" of Hindu legend has a curious parallel in Phœnician mythology. The invention of the Phœnician written character is referred to the god Taaut or Thoth, whose snake-symbol bears his name Têt, and is used to represent the ninth letter of the alphabet (ט *teth*), which in the oldest Phœnician character has the form of the snake curling itself up. Philo thus explains the form of the letter ϑ *theta*, and that the god from whom it took its name was designated by the Egyptians as a serpent curled up, with its head turned inwards. Philo adds that the letters of the Phœnician alphabet "are those formed by means of serpents; afterward, when they built temples, they assigned them a place in the adytums, instituted various ceremonies and solemnities in honor of them, and adored them as the supreme gods, the rulers of the universe." Bunsen thinks the sense of this passage is "that the forms and movements of serpents were employed in the invention of the oldest letters, which represent the gods." He says, however, that "the alphabet does not tally at all with the Phœnician names," and the explanation given by Philo, although curious as showing the ideas anciently associated with the serpent, is reliable only so far as it confirms the connection between that animal and the inventor of the written characters. According to another tradition, the ancient theology of Egypt was said to have been given by the Agathodæmon, who was the benefactor of all mankind.

The account given of the serpent by Sanchoniathon, as cited by Eusebius, is worth repetition as showing the peculiar notions anciently current in connection with that animal. The Phœnician writer says: "Taautus first attributed something divine to the nature of serpents and the serpent-tribe, in which he was followed by the Phœnicians and Egyptians; for this animal was esteemed by him to be the most inspired of all the reptiles, and of a fiery nature, inasmuch as it exhibits an incredible celerity, moving by its spirit without either hands or feet, or any of those external members by which other animals effect their motion, and in its progress it assumes a variety of forms, moving in a spiral course, and darting forwards with whatever degree of swiftness it pleases. It is, moreover, long-lived, and has the quality not only of putting off its old age, and assuming a second youth, but of receiving at the same time an augmentation of its size and strength, and when it has fulfilled the appointed measure of its existence it consumes itself, as Taautus has laid down in the sacred books; upon which account this animal is introduced in the sacred rites and Mysteries." In India, at the present day, some Brahmans always keep the skin of a nâg, or snake, in one of their sacred books, probably from some idea connected with the casting by the serpent of its skin, referred to in the preceding passage.

We have now seen that the serpent was anciently the symbol of wisdom, life, and healing, and also that it was thought to have power over the wind and rain. This last attribute is easily understood when the importance of the rain in the East is considered, and the ideas associated by the ancients with the air and moisture are remembered. The Hebrew tradition which speaks of the creative spirit moving over the face of the waters embodies those ideas, according to which the water contains the elements of life and the wind is the vivifying principle. The attribute of wisdom cannot so easily be connected with that of life. The power of healing is certainly an evidence of the possession of wisdom,* but as it is only one phase of it, probably the latter attribute was antecedent to the former, or at least it may have had an independent origin. What this origin was may perhaps be explained by reference to certain other ideas very generally entertained in relation to the serpent. Among various African tribes this animal is viewed with great veneration, under the belief that it is often the reëmbodiment of a deceased ancestor. This notion appears to be prevalent also among the Hindus, who, like the Kafirs, will never kill a serpent, although it is usually regarded with more dislike than veneration. Mr. Squier remarks that "many of the North American tribes entertain a superstitious regard for serpents, and particularly for the rattlesnake. Though always avoiding they never destroy it, 'lest,' says Barham, 'the spirit of the reptile should excite its kindred to revenge.'" Mr. Squier adds that, "according to Adair, this fear was not unmingled with

* According to Gaelic and Germanic folklore, the white snake when boiled has the faculty of conferring medicinal wisdom. The white snake is venerated as the king of serpents by the Scottish Highlanders as by certain Arab tribes, and it would appear also by the Singhalese of Ceylon.

veneration. Charlevoix states that the Natchez had the figure of a rattlesnake, carved from wood, placed among other objects upon the altar of their temple, to which they paid great honor. Heckwelder relates that the Linni Linape called the rattlesnake 'grandfather,' and would on no account allow it to be destroyed. Hemy states that the Indians around Lake Huron had a similar superstition, and also designated the rattlesnake as their 'grandfather.' He also mentions instances in which offerings of tobacco were made to it, and its parental care solicited for the party performing the sacrifice. Carver also mentions an instance of similar regard on the part of a Menominee Indian, who carried a rattlesnake constantly with him, 'treating it as a deity, and calling it his great father.'" *

The most curious notion, however, is that of the Mexicans, who always represented the first woman, whose name was translated by the old Spanish writers "the woman of our flesh," as accompanied by a great male serpent. This serpent is the sun-god *Tonacatl-coatl*, the principal deity of the Mexican pantheon, and his female companion, the goddess mother of mankind, has the title *cihua-cohuatl*, which signifies "woman of the serpent." With the Peruvians, also, the principal deity was the serpent-sun, whose wife, the female serpent, gave birth to a boy and a girl from whom all mankind were said to be descended. It is remarkable that the serpent-origin thus ascribed to the human race is not confined to the aborigines of America. According to Herodotus, the primeval mother of the Scyths was a monster, half woman and half serpent. This reminds as of the serpent-parentage ascribed to various personages of classical antiquity. Among the Semites, Zohak, the traditional Arabian conqueror of Central Asia, is represented as having two snakes growing at his back; and Mr. Bruce mentions that the line of the Abyssinian kings begins with "The Serpent," *Arwe*, who is said to have reigned at Axum for 400 years, showing that the royal descent was traced from this animal. From the position assigned to the dragon in China, it probably was formerly thought to stand in a similar relation to the Emperor, of whom it is the special symbol.

The facts cited prove that the serpent-superstition is intimately connected with ancestor-worship, probably

* The snake is one of the Indian tribal *totems*.

originating among uncultured tribes who, struck by the noiseless movement and the activity of the serpent, combined with its peculiar gaze and marvellous power of fascination, viewed it as a spirit-embodiment. As such, it would be supposed to have the superior wisdom and power ascribed to the denizens of the invisible world, and from this would originate also the ascription to it of the power over life and health, and over the moisture on which those benefits are dependent. The Serpent-spirit may, however, have made its appearance for a good or a bad purpose, to confer a benefit or to inflict punishment for the misdeeds of the living. The notion of there being good and evil serpent-spirits would thus naturally arise. Among ancestor-worshipping peoples, however, the serpent would be viewed as a good being who busied himself about the interests of the tribe to which he had once belonged. When the simple idea of a spirit-ancestor was transformed into that of the Great Spirit, the father of the race, the attributes of the serpent would be enlarged. The common ancestor would be relegated to the heavens, and that which was necessary to the life and well-being of his people would be supposed to be under his care. Hence the Great Serpent was thought to have power over the rain and the hurricane, with the latter of which he was probably often identified.

When the serpent was thus transferred to the atmosphere, and the superstition lost its simple character as a phase of ancestor-worship, its most natural association would be with the solar cult. It is not surprising, therefore, to find that *Quetzal-coatl*, the divine benefactor of the Mexicans, was an incarnation of the serpent-sun *Tonacatl-coatl*, who thus became the great father, as the female serpent *Cihua-coatl* was the great mother, of the human race. It is an interesting inquiry how far the sun-gods of other peoples partook of this double character. Bunsen has a remarkable passage bearing on the serpent-nature of those deities. He says that "Esmun-Esculapius is strictly a Phœnician god. He was especially worshipped at Berytus. At Carthage he was called the highest god, together with Astartè and Hercules. At Babylon, according to the above genealogy of Bel, Apollo corresponded to him. As the snake-god he must actually be Hermes, in Phœnician Têt, Taautes. . . . In an earlier stage of kosmogonical consciousness he is

Agathodæmon-Sôs, whom Lepsius has shown to be the third god in the first order of the Egyptian Pantheon." The serpent-deity who was thus known under so many forms was none other than the sun-god Set or Saturn, who has already been identified with Siva and other deities having the attributes usually ascribed to the serpent. Bunsen asserts that Set is common to all the Semites and and Chaldæans, as he was to the Egyptians, but that "his supposed identity with Saturn is not so old as his identity with the sun-god, as Sirius (Sôthis), because the sun has the greatest power when it is in Sirius." Elsewhere the same writer says that "the Oriento-Egyptian conception of Typhon-Set was that of a drying-up parching heat. Set is considered as the sun-god when he has reached his zenith, the god of the summer sun."

The solar character of the serpent-god appears therefore to be placed beyond doubt. But what was the relation in which he was supposed to stand to the human race? Bunsen, to whose labors I am so much indebted, remarks that Seth "appears gradually among the Semites as the background of their religious consciousness," and not merely was he "the primitive god of northern Egypt and Palestine," but his genealogy as "the Seth of *Genesis*, the father of Enoch (the man), must be considered as originally running parallel with that derived from the Elohim, Adam's father." Seth is thus the divine ancestor of the Semites; a character in which, but in relation to other races, the solar deities generally agree with him. The kings and priests of ancient peoples claimed this divine origin, and "children of the sun" was the title of the members of the sacred caste. When the actual ancestral character of the deity is hidden he is regarded as "the father of his people" and their divine benefactor. He is the introducer of agriculture, the inventor of arts and sciences, and the civilizer of mankind; "characteristics," says Faber, "which every nation ascribed to the first of their gods or the oldest of their kings." This was true of Thoth, Saturn, and other analogous deities, and the Adam of Hebrew tradition was the father of agriculture, as his representative Noah was the introducer of the vine.

Elsewhere I have endeavored to show that the name of the great ancestor of Hebrew tradition has been preserved by certain peoples who may thus be classed together as Adamites. He appears, indeed, to be the recognised legendary ancestor of the members of that division of mankind whose primeval home we can scarcely doubt was in Central Asia, answering in this respect to the Seth of the Semites. According to the tradition, however, as handed down to us by the Hebrews, Seth himself was the son of Adam. From this, it would seem to follow that, as Seth was the serpent sun-god (the Agathodæmon), the legendary ancestor of the Adamites must himself have partaken of the same character. Strange as this idea may appear it is not without warrant. We have already seen that the Mexicans ascribed that nature to *Tonacatl-coatl* and his wife, the mother of mankind, and that a similar notion was entertained by various peoples of the old world. The Chaldean god *Héa* who, as the "teacher of mankind," and the "lord of understanding," answers exactly to the divine benefactor of the race before referred to, was "figured by the great serpent which occupies so conspicuous a place among the symbols of the gods on the black stones recording Babylonian benefactions." The name of the god is connected with the Arabic *Hiya*, which signifies a serpent as well as life, and Sir Henry Rawlinson says that "there are very strong grounds indeed for connecting him with the serpent of scripture, and with the Paradisaical traditions of the tree of knowledge and the tree of life." The god Héa was, therefore, the serpent-revealer of knowledge, answering in some respects to the serpent of the fall. He, was, however, the Agathodæmon, and in the earlier form of the legend doubtless answered to the great human ancestor himself. It is curious that, according to Rabbinical tradition, Cain was the son, not of Adam, but of the serpent-spirit Asmodeus, who is the same as the Persian Ahriman, "the Great Serpent with two feet." In the name of Eve, the mother of mankind, we have, indeed, direct reference to the supposed serpent-nature of our first parents. Clemens Alexandrinus long since remarked that the name *Hevia*, aspirated, signifies a female serpent. The name Eve is evidently connected with the same Arabic root as that which we have seen to mean both "life" and "a serpent," and the Persians appear to have called the constellation *Serpens* "the little Ava," that is *Eve*, a title which is still given to it by the Arabs. But if Eve was the serpent-mother, Adam must have been the serpent-father. In the old Akkad tongue *Ad* signifies "a father," and the mythical personages with whom Adam is most nearly allied, such as Seth or Saturn, Taaut or Thoth, and others, were serpent-deities.* Such would seem to have been the case also with the deities whose names show a close formal resemblance to that of Adam. Thus the original name of Hercules was *Sandan* or *Adanos*, and Hercules, like the allied god Mars, was undoubtedly often closely associated with the serpent. This notion is confirmed by the identification of Adonis and Osiris as *Azar* or *Adar*, according to Bunsen the later Egyptian *Sar-Apis*, who is known to have been represented as a serpent. The Abaddon of St. John, the old dragon Satan, was probably intended for the same serpent-god. It is interesting to compare the ideas entertained as to the great dragon in the book of *Revelation* and those held by the Chinese in relation to probably the same being. Mr. Doolittle says: "The dragon holds a remarkable position in the history and government of China. It also enjoys an ominous eminence in the affections of the Chinese people. It is frequently represented as the greatest benefactor of mankind. It is the dragon which causes the clouds to form and the rain to fall. The Chinese delight in praising its wonderful properties and powers. It is the venerated symbol of good."

It is remarkable that one of the most ancient people of whom we have any written record—the primitive inhabitants of Chaldæa—not only bore the name of the tradi-

* "Serpents," says Prof. Ch. Gubernatis, "are revered in India as embodied souls of the dead. . . . In Scandinavian mythology, Odin also assumes the form of a serpent in the same way as Zeus becomes a serpent in Greek mythology when he wishes to create Zagreus. In Rockholtz and Simrock, we find indications of the same worship which is given to the serpent in India, where it is regarded as a good domestic genie. Milk is given to certain domestic little snakes to drink; they are put to watch over little children in their cradles. . . . It is fabled, moreover, that a serpent . . . procures for good and beautiful maidens husbands worthy of them. According to a popular legend, two serpents are found in every house (a male and a female), which only appear when they announce the death of the master and mistress of the house; when they die the snakes also cease to live. To kill one of these serpents, is to kill the head of the family. Under this aspect, as a protector of children, as a giver of husbands to girls, and identified with the head or progenitor of the family, the serpent is again a phallical form."

Æneas, it will be remembered, when about to celebrate at the tomb of Anchises the anniversary of his death, was surprised at the appearing of a huge snake that glided among the altars and tasted the banquet, after which it retired to the bottom of the tomb. He did not know whether it was the *genius loci*, or his father's attendant demon.—Virgil: *Æneid*, v. line 84.

tional father of mankind, but were especially identified with the serpent. The predecessors of the *Akkad*, in Chaldæa, were the Medes, or *Mad*, of Berosus, and the distinctive title of at least the later Medes was *Már*, which in Persian means "a snake." This Sir Henry Rawlinson supposes to have given rise "not only to the Persian traditions of Zohák and his snakes, but to the Armenian traditions, also, of the dragon-dynasty of Media." The Medes of Berosus belonged almost certainly to the old Scythic stock of Central Asia, to whom the Chaldæans, the Hebrews, and the Aryans have alike been affiliated by different writers. When, therefore, Mr. Fergusson says that serpent-worship characterised the old Turanian Chaldæan Empire, he would seem to trace it to the old Asiatic centre. Probably to the same source must be traced the serpent-tradition of the Abyssinian kings. Bryant long since asserted that that superstition originated with the Amonians or Hamites, who also would seem to have been derived from the Scythic stock. The facts brought together in this paper far from exhaust the subject, but they appear to justify the following conclusions:—

First, The serpent has been viewed with awe or veneration from primeval times, and almost universally as a reëmbodiment of a deceased human being, and as such there were ascribed to it the attributes of life and wisdom, and the power of healing.

Secondly, The idea of a simple spirit reïncarnation of a deceased ancestor gave rise to the notion that mankind originally sprang from a serpent, and ultimately to a legend embodying that idea.

Thirdly, This legend was connected with nature- or rather sun-worship, and the sun was, therefore, looked upon as the divine serpent-father of man and nature.

Fourthly, Serpent-worship, as a developed religious system, originated in Central Asia, the home of the great Scythic stock, from whom all the civilised races of the historical period sprang.

Fifthly, These peoples are the Adamites, and their legendary ancestor was at one time regarded as the Great Serpent, his descendants being in a special sense serpent-worshippers.

IRELAND'S SHAKSPEARE FORGERIES.

The Confessions of William Henry Ireland, containing the Particulars of his Fabrication of the Shakspeare Manuscripts; together with Anecdotes and Opinions of many Distinguished Persons in the Literary, Political, and Theatrical World. A new edition, with additional Facsimiles, and an Introduction by RICHARD GRANT WHITE. 1 volume 12mo, vellum cloth, uncut edges, $2.00; or on Large and Thick paper, 8vo, $3.50. *Edition limited to 300 copies.*

ORIGINAL LISTS OF PERSONS OF QUALITY.

Emigrants; Religious Exiles; Political Rebels; Servingmen Sold for a Term of Years; Apprentices; Children Stolen; Maidens Pressed; and others who went from Great Britain to the American Plantations, 1600–1700. With their Ages, the Localities where they formerly Lived in the Mother Country, Names of the Ships in which they embarked, and other interesting particulars. From MSS. preserved in the State Paper Department of Her Majesty's Public Record Office, England. Edited by JOHN CAMDEN HOTTEN. A very handsome volume, crown 4to, 700 pages, elegantly bound in half roxburgh morocco, gilt top, $10.00.

A few Large Paper copies have been printed, small folio, $17.50.

THE LOST BEAUTIES OF THE ENGLISH LANGUAGE.

An Appeal to Authors, Poets, Clergymen, and Public Speakers. By CHAS. MACKAY, LL.D. 1 vol. 12mo, cloth extra, $1.75.

This is a perfect treasure of "Lost Beauties." Words change as well as men sometimes from no longer meeting the new wants of the people, but oftener from the attraction of novelty which impels everybody to change. A dictionary of obsolete words, and terms becoming obsolete, is a valuable reminder of the treasures which we are parting with; not always wisely, for in them are comprised a wealth of expression, idiom, and even history, which the new words cannot acquire. Dr. Mackay has placed a host of such on record, with quotations to illustrate how they were read by the classical writers of the English language, not many centuries ago, and enables us to read those authors more understandingly. If he could induce us to recall some of them back to life, it would be a great boon to literature; but hard as it might have been for Cæsar to add a new word to his native Latin language, it would have been infinitely more difficult to resuscitate an obsolete one, however more expressive and desirable. Many of the terms embalmed in this treatise are not dead as yet; and others of them belong to that prolific department of our spoken language that does not get into dictionaries. But we all need to know them; and they really are more homogeneous to our people than their successors, the stilted foreign-born and alien English, that "the Best" is laboring to naturalize into our language. The old words, like old shoes and well-worn apparel, sit most comfortably.

The following mystical pictures are not related to this book.

They have been included for your enjoyment.

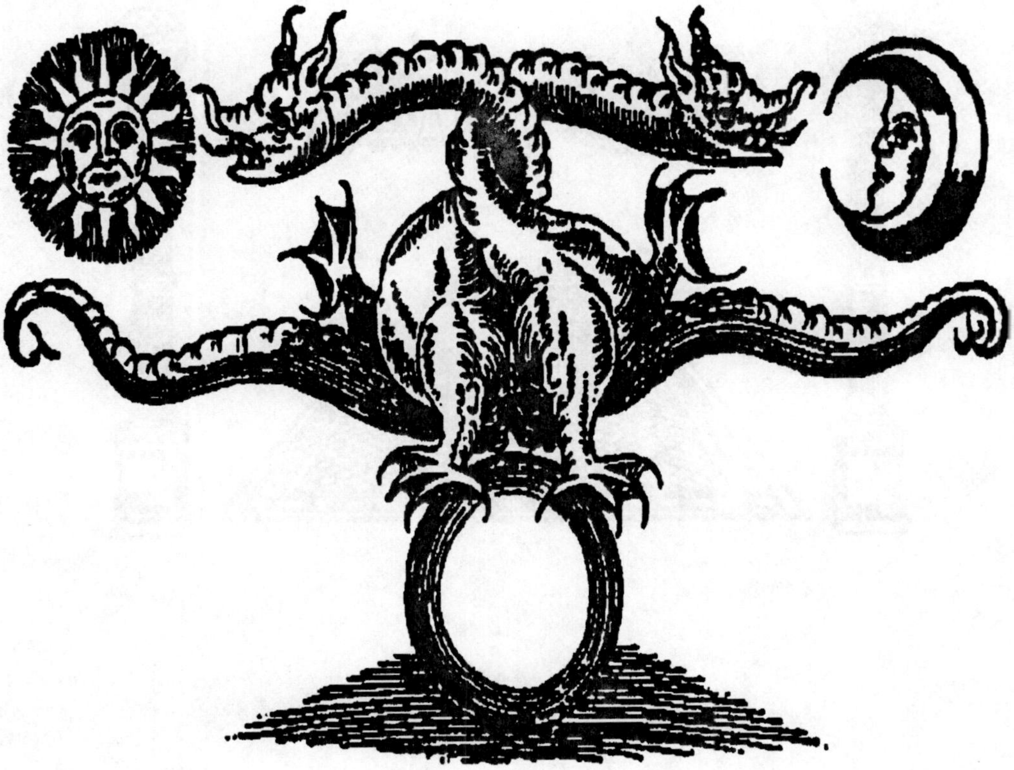

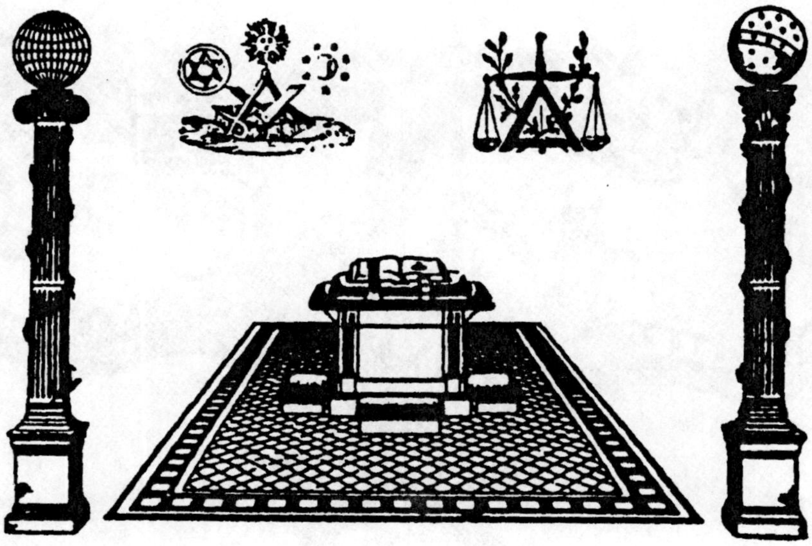

Pictures 2

FAITH, HOPE,
AND
CHARITY.

Pictures 4

Pictures 5

ALCHYMIA

(From Thurneysser's *Quinta Essentia*, 1570)

Pictures 7

Pictures 8

Pictures 9

Assyrian Type of Gilgamesh

Pictures 11

PARABRAHM
LOGOS
LIGHT
ILLUSION

MASONIC APRON PRESENTED TO GEN. WASHINGTON
BY MADAME LAFAYETTE.

THE GOLDEN WHEEL

Pictures 15

Pictures 16

Pictures 17

Pictures 18

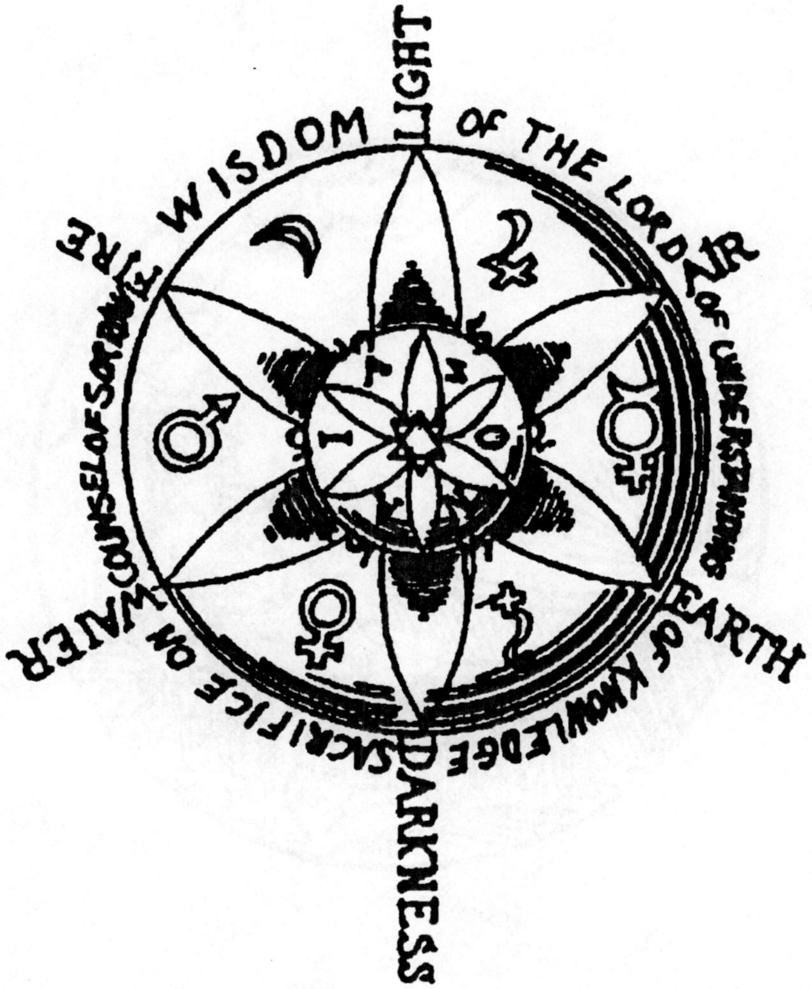
WISDOM
LIGHT
OF THE LORD
AIR
OF UNDERSTANDING
EARTH
OF KNOWLEDGE
DARKNESS
SACRIFICE
WATER
COUNSEL OF SORROW
FIRE

Pictures 19

Pictures 20

OBEISSEZ A VOS SUPERIEURS ET LEUR SOYEZ SOUMIS PARCE QU'ILS·Y PRENNENT GARDE
B

Pictures 22

Pictures 23

Pictures 24

IMMA
NUEL
IN HOC
SIGNO
VINCES

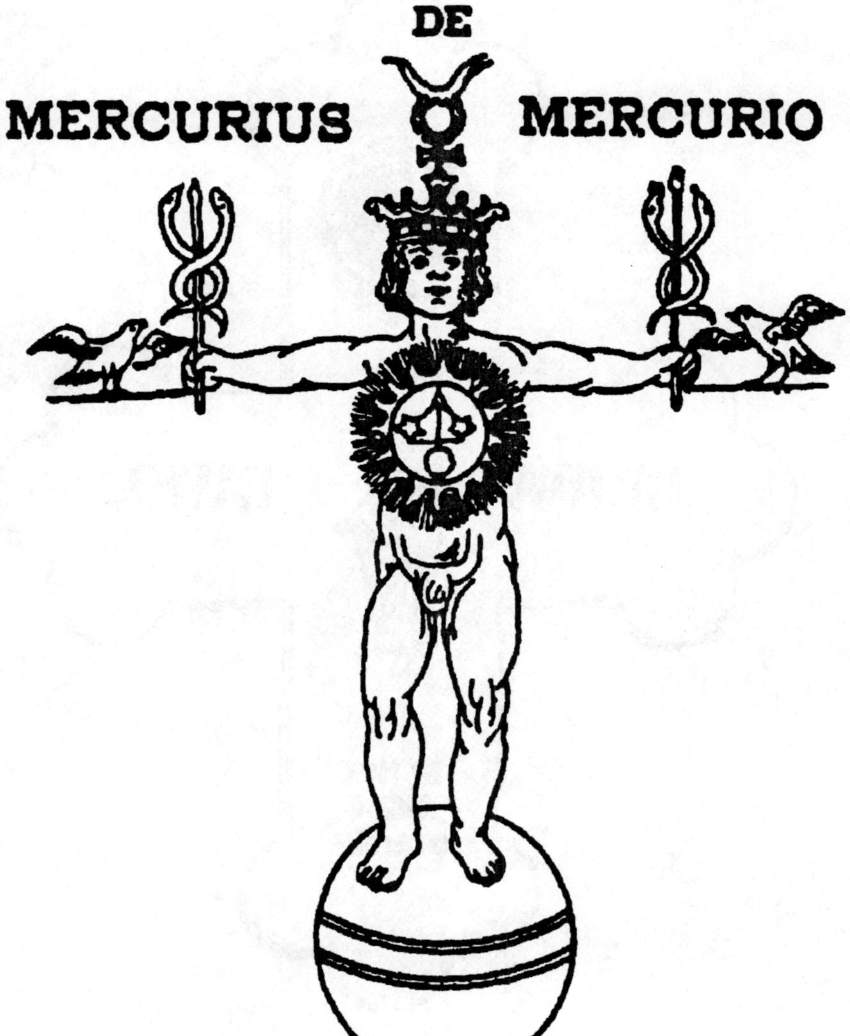
DE
MERCURIUS
MERCURIO

Father
Son
H.Ghost
FIAT
NAT URA
Omnia
ab Uno

Pictures 28

Pictures 29

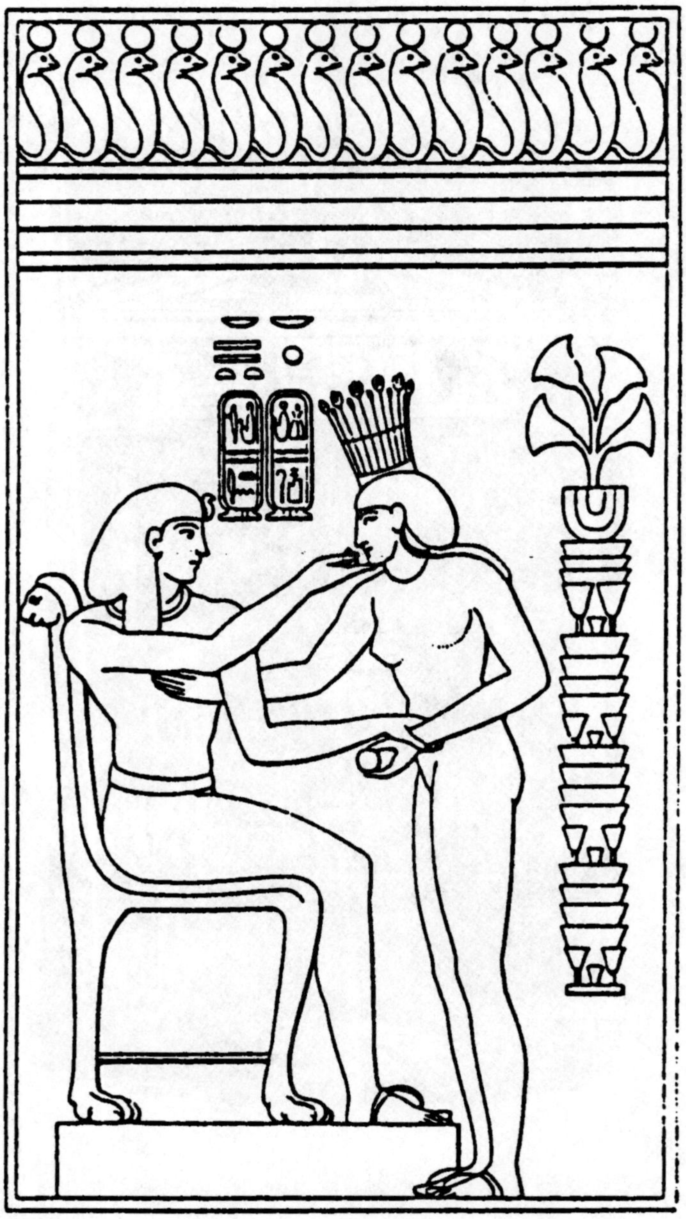

Pictures 30

ע
ס
ג
ל
י
ט
ח
ז
ו
ה
ק
צ
ב
פ
א
ש
מ

Pictures 33

Pictures 34

DAT ROSA MEL APIBUS.

Pictures 36

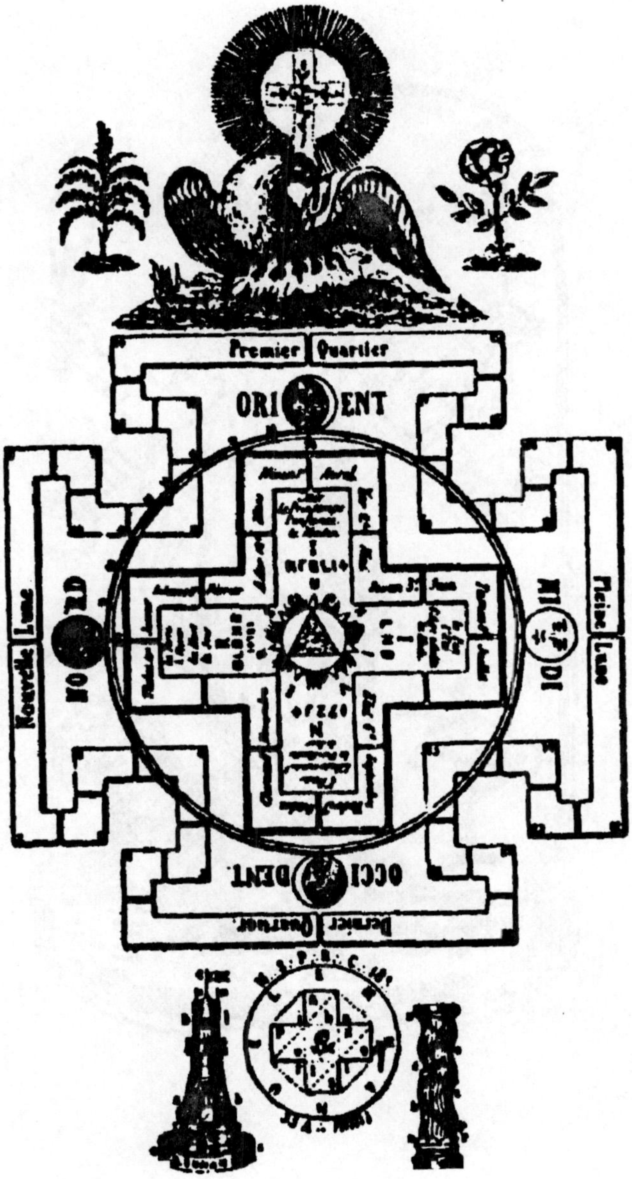
Premier Quartier
ORI ENT
OCCI DENT.
Dernier Quartier
Nouvelle Lune
Pleine Lune

ADDA-NARI

Pictures 40

Pictures 41

GLORIOR
ELATUS
AD ALTA
VEHOR
AXI
ROTOR
DESCENDO
MORTIFICAT9
FORTUNA

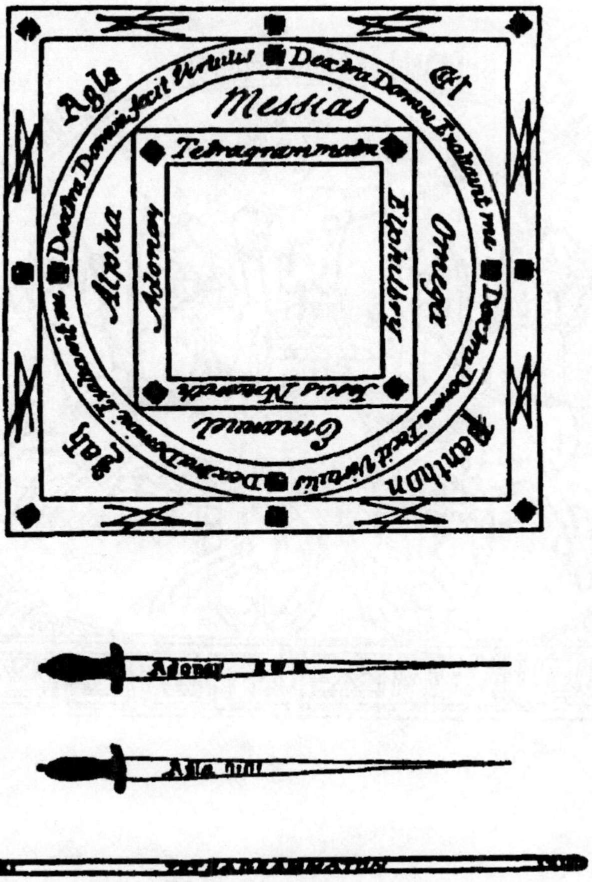

THE MAGIC CIRCLE AND WEAPONS.

Pictures 44

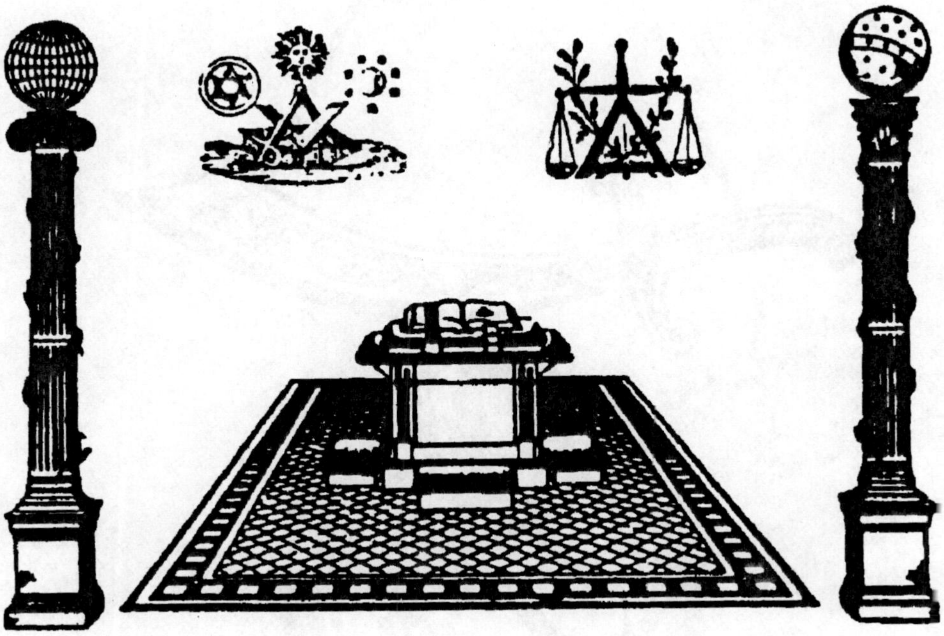

Pictures 45

Pictures 46

Pictures 47

Pictures 48

Pictures 49

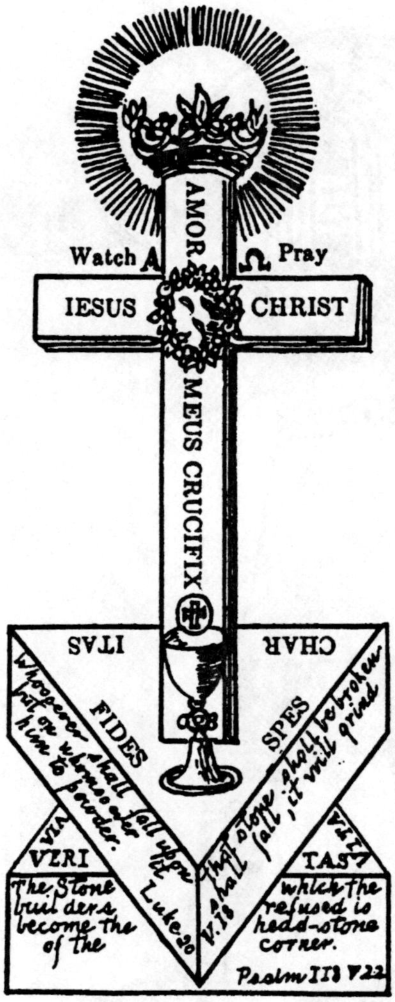

Watch
Pray
IESUS
CHRIST
AMOR MEUS CRUCIFIX
CHAR
ITAS
FIDES
SPES
VIA
VERI
TAS
VITA
Whosoever shall fall upon it
but on whomsoever
him to powder.
Luke 20
that stone shall be broken
shall fall, it will grind
V.18
The Stone
builders
become the
of the
which the
refused is
head-stone
corner.
Psalm 118 V22

Printed in the United Kingdom
by Lightning Source UK Ltd.
99169UKS00001B/1